NEVER DOUBT
THAT A SMALL GROUP
OF THOUGHTFUL COMMITTED CITIZENS
CAN CHANGE THE WORLD:
INDEED,
IT IS THE ONLY THING,
THAT EVER HAS.
—Margaret Mead

IMAGINATION IS MORE IMPORTANT THAN
KNOWLEDGE.
—Einstein

HELLO, BABIES. WELCOME TO EARTH.
IT'S HOT IN THE SUMMER AND COLD IN THE WINTER.
IT'S ROUND AND WET AND CROWDED.
AT THE OUTSIDE, BABIES, YOU'VE GOT
ABOUT A HUNDRED YEARS HERE.
THERE'S ONLY ONE RULE
THAT I KNOW OF, BABIES:
"GOD DAMN IT, YOU'VE GOT TO BE KIND."
—Kurt Vonnegut, Jr.

If there is no struggle,
there is no progress.
Those who profess to favor freedom
and yet renounce controversy
are people who want crops
without ploughing the ground.
—Frederick Douglass

Witches Heal
HUGS HEAL
—buttons and bumper stickers

I touch the future.
I teach.
—Anonymous

Sing! Feast! Dance!
You who would learn...I will teach you.
—the Charge of the Goddess

Raising Witches

Teaching the Wiccan Faith to Children

By
Ashleen O'Gaea

New Page BOOKS

A division of The Career Press, Inc.
Franklin Lakes, NJ

Copyright © 2002 by Ashleen O'Gaea

RAISING WITCHES

EDITED AND TYPESET BY KATE PRESTON

Cover design by Cheryl Cohan Finbow

Printed in the U.S.A. by Book-mart Press

To order this title, please call toll-free 1-800-CAREER-1 (NJ and Canada: 201-848-0310) to order using VISA or MasterCard, or for further information on books from Career Press.

The Career Press, Inc., 3 Tice Road, PO Box 687, Franklin Lakes, NJ 07417

www.careerpress.com
www.newpagebooks.com

Library of Congress Cataloging-in-Publication Data

O'Gaea, Ashleen.
    Raising witches : teaching the Wiccan faith to children / by Ashleen O'Gaea.
        p. cm.
    Includes bibliographical references and index.
    ISBN 1-56414-631-6 (pbk.)
    1. Witchcraft. 2. Family—Religious life. 3. Child rearing—Religious aspects—Goddess religion. 4. Goddess religion. I. Title.

BF1572.F35 O355 2002
299—dc21

2002071930

Dedication

To Canyondancer and the Explorer;
and to Blanche—the Grandmother Teacher.

Contents

Preface	13
Introduction	15
Regency Parenting	21
Passage Rights	25
What' a Kid Ready to Learn About Wicca?	32
Infancy	35
What Babies Need Most	38
Ivy's Song	50
Early Childhood	53
Young Children's Anger	56
Mythical Children	57
Patience, Please	71
Magical Security	73
Cakes and Ale and Children	76
Making a Robe	78
The Wheel of the Year	80
How Spells Work	87

Later Childhood   **91**

Keeping Secrets   95

Animal Associations   98

Plant Associations   102

Teaching corrspondences Through
Word Games   102

Questions Religions Address   104

Skyclad Children   108

Acorns Don't Provide Shade   110

Adolescence   **117**

The Mirror in the Meadow   121

The Wiccan Rede   126

Guilt Trips   129

Making Commitments   131

Advantages of Guided Meditations   132

Young Adulthood   **141**

     The War Against Children   145

     The Retreat   150

     Your First Book of Shadows   158

     Religion and Politics   162

     Self-Dedication   166

Sun Day School   **167**

     Before You Print the Flyers   173

     Saying No   174

     Reinforcing Your Lessons   182

     Later Childhood: Syllabus for six sessions: 188

     Sample Lesson Plan: Session Three   190

Glossary   **193**

Bibliography and Recommended Readings   **207**

Index   **211**

About the Author   **217**

Preface

This book is written for people who want to teach Wicca to children in a more or less formal way. However, by "formal," we don't mean "sit perfectly still and only listen," we mean "deliberately." We—my husband and High Priest (HHP), Canyondancer, and I—have heard from many who want to schedule classes at regular times and make lesson plans, and this book will help you do that, but it offers support for different learning structures, too.

There is a fine line between "parenting Wiccan" and "teaching Wicca," and quite often, parent and teacher are the same person. In all cases, parents are assumed to be aware that they teach, and teachers are assumed to care about their students more deeply and personally than most secular teachers can these days. (In secular society , it doesn't happen very often that one's kindergarten teacher also passes out one's high school or college diploma, but that is essentially what happens in many Pagan communities: children are eventually initiated by the same people who've been teaching them "since forever.")

This book is also for people curious about how Wicca might be taught to children. We've heard from people who aren't Wiccan, but who care about children who are, and who need to allay their concerns about Wicca's content and style. In addition, this book is for educators in any subject who'd like to enhance their courses.

Another thing I need to make clear is that we are Wiccan, and have lived and written this book from our experience in this denomination of the Craft, there are Traditions of Wicca other than ours and other Pagan religions as well. Even though our examples are from our coven and the experiences we've had in Tucson, the approach to religious education presented here is effective and appropriate for most Pagans (of any Trad or religion) to use in teaching their own material and customs. Indeed, we encourage all Pagans to join the growing number of Wiccans in restoring the Old Religions for our children and the world.

Finally, on a couple of mundane notes: Sexism is awful, and we don't like it, and so when possible I've used "they" and "their" and other plural forms (children, teachers, etc.) in an effort to keep it gender-free or -neutral. The material in this book is for students (and teachers) of either gender or any orientation.

This book was written over the course of a few years. Canyondancer's name isn't on the cover, but his influence on this book—not to mention in our son's life and our local Pagan community—is strong. It's been his quiet dedication and old-fashioned hard work that have made our most wonderful experiences possible. Our son, the Explorer, is grown now and he no longer camps with us or practices Wicca, but continues to be both respectful of the faith (he's often our still and video photographer) and of the Earth and all its lives, including his parents and their wacky friends. Without the Explorer by our sides or covering our backs, quite a few of our most wonderful experiences would have been less wonderful. We still think parenting is the neatest thing there is.

Strength through Diversity. Blessed be.

Introduction

For years we were asked, when people discovered that we were Witches, whether we were raising our son according to the Craft. When we said we were doing so, we were asked whether we thought that was "wise." We always smiled and said we were sure it was. We are still sure that it was, and is, "wise" to teach our children the Neo-Pagan religions we practice.

Yet, for a number of reasons, many Wiccans wonder the same thing: should we? dare we? Now, some of us were forcibly taught our parents' religions, and we quite reasonably shy from "doing that" to our own children. Knowing that it is everyone's inherent right to choose their own faith, some of us don't teach children about Wicca so as not to compromise their freedom. And a lot of us just **don't know how** to teach Wicca to our children.

In this book, we'll integrate a framework for lessons in Wicca with what's known about the way children grow up. For five stages of development (infancy, early childhood, late childhood, adolescence, and young adulthood) we'll look at some passage rites and explore the possibilities for spells and rituals. We'll talk about the guided experiences parents and other teachers can offer children of any age; and we'll be talking about our own inner children as well as our offspring and students.

Being an experiential religion, Wicca is holistic, embracing our feelings as well as our reason. This means that it's appropriate to *teach* Wicca with respect for feelings and with expectations of reason. Actually, it is impossible to teach Wicca by force! It can't be "rammed down" anyone's throat because...there are no threats to make, no punishments to promise.

Some gods are admittedly jealous, but Wicca's Lady and Lord are loving partners to each other, and loving mentors (among other things) to us. We're accountable for our mistakes, and expected to learn from them, but we don't believe that making mistakes makes us unlovable to deity. We may have *heard* "God will get you for that!" but we can't say it to our children or students because in Wicca, it's not true.

Wicca is a personal faith: a belief system based on experience and confirmation. Because humans are social creatures, much of our experience is with our fellow humans and we are encouraged and even inspired when our fellows affirm our perceptions. As babies, our sense of trust is strengthened when we smile and somebody smiles back at us; even grown-ups think that trust feels good.

When we find that other people believe what we believe, see the world the way we do, we are empowered. (This explains the "coming home" feeling most Witches get when they discover Wicca.) That's why we think it's good to teach our children about Wicca. Our philosophy of religious education will appear throughout this book, and while it's great if you agree with most of what you read, what I really hope is that you'll think about *your* ideas about why and how to teach Wicca to the children in your life. There's no such thing as "not teaching" our children. The only question is *what* we're going to teach; the only answer we know for sure is that we'll teach them more, and maybe differently, than what we think we're teaching them.

Before the Explorer was born, we read all the child development books we could get our hands on. Some of our friends teased us about that, thinking we were "intellectualizing" parenting. These days, more of us are without the extended family that supported young or first-time parents before the middle of the 20th century, and we need all the help we can get!

It's good to be willing to learn new things—at least that's what we tell our children, isn't it? It's good to be able to make use of new information to enhance your life. Even people who are "naturals" benefit from a bit of instruction, discipline, and coaching. It has to do with being a social species: we're actually hard-wired to learn from, and about, virtually everything we do! So, we can say to anyone worried about it, or critical of it, there's no shame in reading this and other books for background information so that your parenting has support. We encourage you to check out the books listed in the Bibliography.

The books we found most useful were those that told us how the child's brain develops. The ones we liked best said things such as: *At the same time they can put the differently-shaped blocks in the right holes on the sides of the toy, they're ready to....* We've integrated much of what we learned from these books, from our experience, and from all the PBS shows we've watched, with some solidly Wiccan material appropriate to every age-group.

Whether you use this material to begin organizing "Sun Day School" or "Moon School" (as it's been dubbed in Tucson) for the children in your Pagan community, to enrich and balance what your own children learn at school, to be more sensitive as a grown-up, or to enrich your own study of Neo-Paganism, you'll find it sensible and easy to use. (Don't think you have to sit everybody down at 9 a.m. on Sunday morning to teach Wicca to the children: a community's Festivals and picnics, Sabbats and Esbats, camping trips, casual barbecues, and a thousand other places and moments can be your classrooms; and sometimes, the children are the teachers.)

The Tucson Area Wiccan-Pagan Network (TAWN) has sponsored a "Moon School" on and off for several years. One of the difficulties TAWN's program faces is its once-a-month schedule. It is difficult to present a conventional religious education program when there are so few meetings in a year and so much time between them. Finding appropriate meeting sites and arranging a schedule that works for all the chauffeuring parents isn't the only challenge. The concern many parents hold from their own "Sunday School" experience is still great, and even in a long-established community such as Tucson's, there's some wariness.

In any diverse community, there's the question of what to teach the children. Our opinion is that children should be taught their parents' religions, so if most of a community is Wiccan, Wicca should be emphasized. Should other Pagan religions be ignored? Certainly not! It's very important for our children to be not only aware of Neo-Pagan diversity, but to appreciate it, and find strength in that diversity. In Tucson, for instance, there are active Asatru and Druid communities, and we think older children should be introduced to those religions, too—once they're grounded in Wicca.

Grounding your children in the thealogy, cosmology, and ethics of Wicca won't keep them from understanding other religions. On the contrary, it's what will create the context in which they can study other religions and make some sense of them, when they're old enough to make those explorations. *Something* has to be the religious "norm" for our children, and we think Wicca should be the norm for children in Wiccan families.

Our children need to know that there are lots of other Pagan religions—non-Western ones—that are quite different from ours, and they need to understand how other Pagan religions relate to Wicca. But, we believe, children *first* need to know what "we" believe, "we" being their family. Giving all Neo-Pagan religions the same emphasis is usually well-meant—but we think it's a mistake because it offers confusion when children are looking for solid answers. (Children may not fully grasp abstract comparisons until they're adolescents.)

Teaching our children Neo-Pagan religions is not a guarantee that they'll "stay Wiccan" when they grow up. But—if our preparation and presentations are taken seriously—it lets them make future decisions based on the truth about Wicca. I find it hard to understand *not* sharing our beliefs, even if our children can't fully understand them right away. (Children can recognize "special" before they can appreciate it rationally.) Raising our children according to Wicca grounds them in ethical principles that will serve them forever and it creates a special bond between parent and child that will help keep the differences that tend to challenge Westerners as we and our children journey through the years in perspective.

If you teach Wicca consistent with its principles, bearing in mind that what we put into the world returns to us threefold, you will teach patiently and respectfully, paying as much attention to your students as you expect them to pay to you. You will encourage your students to find examples and lessons in their own experiences, and you'll help them develop and learn to trust their intuitions and inspirations. You will let them know that even in a relatively free-wheeling, mostly eclectic religion such as Wicca, as in life itself, there is a structure to support us all.

Thus, we believe, we will meet our major responsibility as adults: to raise the children in our family or community to accountable independence. But there is another responsibility we notice *as Wiccans*, and that is to advance our children through the Craft and the Craft through our children.

When we say "advance our children through the Craft," we mean spare them the time and trouble of growing up shame-based, as many of us did; spare them all the superstition and mistrust we may have had to cope with. Compare it to a committee's brainstorming and coming up with lots of ideas, but only presenting the good ones to the rest of the group. Advance with the good ideas first; there'll be time to tell tales of the bad ones later.

When we say, "advance the Craft through our children," we mean filling them with Wicca's presumptions of belonging and personal authority, and with social, political, and economic expectations that people will learn in order to get along with the rest of the planet. (Aleister Crowley, who first wrote the Rede for Neo-Pagans, was pretty specific that if people actually had a clue about their true Wills, everybody could realize their true callings and nobody would need to get in anybody's way, and all of life would be in harmony. We think he's entirely right about that.) We need to impress that potential on our children so that their expectations of responsibility and peace are "second nature" to them. Then, perhaps, for our children's children, or *their* children, it can get back to being *first* nature.

In focusing on sanctifying—at least mythifying—many mundane experiences, we hope to lay a foundation for the future. (You're "mythifying" something when you perceive it as symbolic of universal concerns. Just like analyzing the meaning of poetry in literature class.) The integration of religious attitudes with "mundane" life is just as important to teach as specific thealogy and ritual are. The division of life into the either/or categories of sacred and profane (mundane) is not one most Witches accept. It is one that needs transforming.

There is one caution to be given here: By teaching Wicca to children, you risk changing the world. It's not just that their *habits* will be different when they're grown, it's that their *expectations* will be different than those we call mainstream today. Pagan-raised people won't accept brutality and callousness, and their demands will be for healthier relationships with each other and the rest of life. Ultimately, this could evolve our cultures and environments to peace and balance! With that caveat, this book is written for, and dedicated to, all those in our communities who teach our children.

O'Gaea & Canyondancer
Blessings from Tucson
Summer 1993 C.E. to Bride-tide 2002 C.E.

Regency Parenting

In this book, we introduce you to a new (well, newly articulated in a Wiccan context) approach to raising children. We offer the concept of parents as their children's *regents*; and naturally enough, we call this *regency parenting*. You'll find its principles woven through everything you read in these pages.

In the Middle Ages, high-born children were fostered in other families, both so they wouldn't take too much advantage of their social positions too soon, and so they could learn the various skills they'd need when they grew up. It was the foster family's job to provide that for those children.

These days, of course, although our children are all most excellent, we don't foster them as a matter of course. We parents now take it upon ourselves to teach our children what they need to know about the worlds. And to what end? So that they will grow up to be responsible and creative, and follow their bliss as adults. To achieve this, though, we have to deliberately give up the power we have over our children when they are born.

We can all remember our own parents' occasional reluctance to let us go when it was time. Witches have fewer excuses than other parents, we think, because we profess respect for the cycle of life. That means (among other things) we have to celebrate our children's coming into their own. With the stereotypical weeping mommy seeing her little one off to kindergarten (or college) still one of our social icons, it can get tricky. Regency parenting reminds us that the whole *point* is to raise another adult.

Conventional parenting focuses on the son's or daughter's obligations to the family, and on the parents' power over the children. Many of us can recall families more concerned with what the neighbors might think than with family members' feelings. Virtually everyone's heard their feelings challenged or denied: "You don't really mean that." Many of us have parents who refuse to recognize that we've grown up and still treat us like small children; plenty of us end up feeling like little children the moment we have to spend any time with our older relatives.

Regency parenting focuses on the son's or daughter's task of growing up, of self-actualizing, as modern psychologists might put it: in the 1960s we called it "finding ourselves." It's still important, and it's part of our job as parents to make sure our children have plenty of experience with their own power. We only hold "our" power over them in trust. When they're babies, they can't do for themselves, so we must. As they get older, they can do more and more—including make mistakes and learn from them—and we must "let" them, just as we let them plop down on their diaper-cushioned bottoms countless times while they learn to walk.

The rest of it involves providing opportunity and experience for them. Even when they're out of diapers we retain some capacity to cushion their blows, but we can't do it physically forever. We have to keep safety in mind, of course, but it's easy to get paranoid, and sometimes it is hard to know what's going to do your children more good than harm. Informing your best guesses with information from several sources is the easiest way to avoid unrealistic worry.

How do we give our children experience so wide that they can draw on it for the rest of their lives, remembering it with pleasure and feeling it resonate with what they do later on, on their own? Canyondancer and I, and a good many of our fellow parents and priests or priestesses, begin with the premise that raising children is magical. To us, this means that we need to prepare ourselves for it carefully, just as we prepare carefully to work any other magic. When we talk to people about children in the Craft, we give the following advice:

Know your intent: like any other magic, parenting needs a goal. (Ours was that the Explorer would be capable of living on his own by the time he was 18, whether or not he actually moved out by then. He stayed with us a little longer, which delighted us, because *we* could hardly wait to get out of our parents' houses.)

Know the appropriate correspondences: read everything you can about child development. Watch all the PBS and cable shows you can about it, too, and demand good scholarship of it all.

You are your child's first Circle, so draw yourself carefully, and be careful what you bring in. Be careful what you let other people bring in, too.

Give the Goddess and God room and time to work. Our bodies mature about 10 years earlier than our brains do. Our brains need more time to grow up because humans rely on learning, and there's lots to learn (and more every generation). Be patient and hang in there.

Your relationship to your children is a magic spell. Take as much care in its phrasing as you would in putting quill and dragon's blood ink to parchment. Be sure that your language is appropriate, not only to the lessons, but to your child's understanding.

Your energy will need raising, and your children's will need grounding. Do these things in celebration and thanksgiving for the blessing of family. By the way, children need to be told straight out that if they *ever* have a problem with other adults, if there's *ever* harassment or worse, that they may, can, should, and must come to you immediately, and you will stand by them. Not without checking it out, but *even* if it disrupts things. *Even* if they name friends of yours and you don't want to believe it. Even if.

The success of parenting magic depends on our ability to see Them manifest in everything. You can't guarantee that your children will grow up to be Witches, yet anything you teach them of the Craft will steady them on any path (every path) they take.

There may be no more royal courts whereat to foster our children so they can learn high culture, but there are museums, maybe in the arts district, maybe at a nearby university. Beyond that, there are theaters, concerts, and lectures. (The more trouble you must take to share any of these cultural resources with your children, the more value they will understand these experiences to have.)

Marketplaces, so long the meeting place for common folk, are not gone, and there are arts and crafts fairs, and Renaissance Faires— not to mention Pagan gatherings in most parts of the country. The annual Fall Fest of the Tucson Area Wiccan-Pagan Network (TAWN) always includes children's activities and encourages children to be part of the open Mabon rite that ends the day.

No more tales of fantastic beasts in foreign lands? Just check your local PBS listings, or take a trip to your local zoo. There are wild animal parks and local pet shows to visit; check out arboretums, too. Sometimes city or county parks host nature walks or slide shows; and don't be afraid to learn about local flora and fauna and create your own nature walk. Keep camping in mind, too.

If there's a planetarium nearby, the sky's the limit! Planetarium programs can range from the latest we've learned from high-tech space travel to what the ancients saw in the constellations. At most planetariums, the accompanying permanent exhibits are pretty interesting too, and at some, there are hands-on displays for children of all ages.

On short trips around town, tell stories about buildings you've never been inside, wonder what goes on, guess—one day, you might even stop and find out, if they're open to the public. Slow down when you pass beautiful gardens or interesting architecture. Watch the local paper for stories about interesting local folk, and make an effort to meet them. (In the vernacular, we might say that the rule is to *blow nothing off.*)

On longer trips, be aware that all adventurers deal with the same problems: deciding how to get there, finding food and shelter on the way, passing the time, getting along with your companions, and brushing up on the local customs. Whether we're focused on this weekend's car trip or this incarnation's journey through life, our ways of coping can enhance the adventure as long as we're aware we're on one.

As we guide our children through the long trips their bodies take while growing up, we can not only help them interpret what's happening today, but also give them a heads up about what they can expect tomorrow. Big changes and strong feelings can be scary, but in safe and trustworthy company, it's safe to acknowledge and experience them fully. As we get taller, we can reach the light switches by ourselves; as we get older, we learn to like other foods; as our brains mature, we understand new things *and* familiar things better.

Passage Rites

Just as important as introducing children to a wide variety of physical and social experiences is giving them some experience with other worlds, including their own inner landscape. Much of what you read in the following pages will be about the process of doing just that. Passage rites can, among other things, encourage—astrally at first—children to do their inner work

If you don't follow a Tradition that has specific passage rites, you'll want to create your own. Most passage rites follow the same Order of Circle that any ritual does, though the details will depend more specifically on the person whose coming of age is being celebrated. Following are a few ideas and examples for you to work with.

A Blessing for Parents and the Soon-to-Arrive

If you can get friends to read this blessing over you and your partner while you're pregnant, it will become a beautiful ceremony even if you don't cast a Circle to do it. If you make it part of a Circle, it will have all the more power in your lives.

By Air and Fire and Water and Earth

may you have an easy birth!

By Winds that blow and gently breathe,

may you weave of Baby's childhood a victory wreath.

By flames of love and passions all

find the courage to rise when you fall.

By stream and ocean, rain and well,

may you always feel family, wherever you dwell.

By highest mountains and valleys low,

may you never fear to let Baby grow.

Blest by East and South and West and North,

as Mom and Dad go, and Baby comes, forth.

May your resources be wide and deep as you undertake this daring thing:

may the Spirit relax you so you can just enjoy parenting!

Wiccaning

When we bring our children into the protection and care of our Wiccan family, whether that's a coven or a loose association of friends (or both), we call it a Wiccaning. This ritual introduces the child to the Quarters, and the God and Goddess, and blessings for the child are given from each of the Quarters and received as well from the Goddess and God, however the group names them. (Lord and Lady are popular titles, for this ritual takes place before a child can meet and have his or her own favorites among Their many aspects.) Here are blessings from

Campsight's Book of Shadows. As with the other ritual elements in this book, use them as they are or modify them to work better for you.

Hail, Old Ones of the East! Hail, Guardians of Air!

Bless this child, name of child, with a vision as wide as the Wind's,

and with the courage of curiosity,

that he (she) may ever greet new dawns without fear.

Hail, Old Ones of the South! Hail, Guardians of Fire!

Bless this child, ____, with a heart as fiery as the Sun,

and the courage of passion,

that she (he) may ever dance in the light without fear.

Hail, Old Ones of the West! Hail, Guardians of Water!
Bless this child, ____, with a soul as deep as the Sea,
and with the courage of love,
that he (she) may ever watch a sunset without fear.

Hail, Old Ones of the North! Hail, Guardians of Earth!
Bless this child, ____, with bones as sturdy as the Earth,
and the courage of commitment,
that she (he) may ever explore the Mystery without fear.

Campsight's Wiccaning, if it's done as part of a Sabbat Circle, comes between the Ale and the Cakes. If it's done on its own, Cakes and Ale are optional (unless the child is old enough for solid food, and then Cake is too much fun to pass up). If they're included, they follow the baby's "Wiccaning lap" around the Circle. Here's an outline.

Parents bring the child in from the Northeast to a fully-cast Circle; the Priest welcomes them and asks for the child's name (magical or civil, parents' choice), and the Priestess recognizes the child by that name. The parents are then charged, and pledge, to teach the child "of the Lady and the Lord, of this life and all that came before, and all that is yet to come." The blessings of the Goddess and God are then asked upon the child. Afterward, the baby is taken to each Quarter for its blessing (which usually manifests in a small gift as well as in words). The baby's recognized as "worthy and entitled to our hospitality and protection." The Sign of the Intertwined Hearts is made over the baby, and more blessings are spoken, ending with the Tradition's blessing. Finally, if there are no objections from the baby, s/he's lifted over Mom's or Dad's head and carried around the Circle once or twice.

"Birthdaying"

Beyond Wiccaning, one of Campsight's priestesses, Chandra Nelson, has written birthday rites for her young daughter. The ritual empowers three stones for the child: a smooth crystal, a piece of jet, and a piece of amethyst. The adults who are chosen to bless each stone for the birthday girl speak these lines:

Crystal:

> I empower this stone to attract all powers wondrous and good. May it empower her to take this next step in her journey.

Jet:

> I empower this stone to absorb all negative forces acting upon this child and those who care for her. May it encompass all negative energies, leaving her path clear for success.

Amethyst:

> As this stone represents the child, let it draw positive energies, love, light, and health. As the Wheel turns, may her coming year be blessed with happiness and gifts from the Lord and Lady.

Dedication

We speak a lot about Self-Dedication, but not every Dedication is "self" or meant to be a covenless First Degree. Younger children usually don't have the resources or experience to produce a ritual meaningful in grown-up terms, yet they are sometimes ready to make some commitment to Wiccan principles. The Explorer "took a Dedication" when he was 7. In the backyard with the men of our community, he accepted responsibility appropriate to his age, and he has never yet abrogated it. Acting as regents, we all need to help our children or students recognize their own growth, and doing so ritually can make a big impression. Children who take to the idea of a Dedication at this age often have pretty clear ideas about how the ritual should go, and as much as possible, they should direct it. After all, they're the ones making the commitment!

Manning and Womaning

A young person ready for a "Manning" or a "Womaning," as our community tends to call these ceremonies, may or may not be ready for an Initiation. That is, and should be, up to the teaching priestess(es) or priest(s) and the student (without leaving the parents out of the loop). Although our rituals might suggest it, there is no single moment at which any of us become an adult. Some passage rites—Queening, for instance (introduced by Z Budapest) and the corresponding Kinging—are usually scheduled when everyone's been aware of the candidate's eligibility for some time. Other rites of passage are commonly set for as soon as possible after some biological event or the attainment of a designated age (often 13, 14, or 21).

Generally, such rites of passage parallel an Initiation ceremony, but it's important to remember that a Manning or Womaning is not the same thing as an Initiation. Initiation recognizes, among other things, the mastery of a certain body of lore and skills, and a concomitant acceptance of the responsibility of coven membership and priest\esshood in the Tradition. Womanings and Mannings recognize that a child is ready to move into an adult role in the community, even though the new adult has much to learn about adulthood. Being a grown-up (according to more than just your age) takes a lot of hard work and practice. A Manning or a Womaning affirms that another young person has stepped onto the Path, but it doesn't presume that they going to reach a destination by morning. It also lets the youngster know that there are safe, same-gendered adults to go to with questions and problems—in a sense, all the men or women

present at a Wiccan child's coming of age become that child's
God/dess-parent.

In this and other respects, "puberty rites" (gosh, doesn't
that sound more pediatric than poetic?) are more like Wiccanings
than Initiations. Those attending, including the Quarters and
the Gods, are unilaterally promising to bless this particular young
person, without expecting any commitment in return. The teen
at the center of a Manning or Womaning rite may wish to make
a commitment, but it's not mandatory. Indeed, we'd recommend
keeping the "puberty rites" separate from any other religious
ritual going on at about the same time, just so the children can
enjoy the "gift" aspect of the bodily changes they're marking.

The following are Campsight's "Coming of Age Quarters"
samples:

> I am the Voice of the East, the white [use your own Quarter color
> correspondences] voice of beginnings, come to inspire your mind. From the
> mountains, from the dawn, I offer you the gift of Intellect. Will you accept my
> gift and ever use it wisely?

> I am the Voice of the South, the red voice of passion, come to
> commit your spirit. From the plains, from the blazing noon, I offer you the gift
> of courage. Will you accept my gift, and ever use it wisely?

> I am the Voice of the West, the blue voice of mystery and intuition,
> come to prepare your soul. From the seas, out of the dusk, I offer you the gifts
> of compassion and empathy. Will you accept my gifts and ever use them
> wisely?

> I am the Voice of the North, the green voice of the Earth, come to
> prepare your body. From the mountains, from the midnight, I offer you the gift
> of strength. Will you accept my gift and ever use it wisely?

In our, and I think most, Traditions, this ritual is restricted
to adults of the same gender as the youngster, but ensuing celebration isn't. To go with these blessings, Quarter Keepers should
have some appropriate natural tokens—perhaps a feather for
East, a flower for South, a shell for West, and a stone for North.

The child transitioning should be given a nice box, or bag, or pouch to keep these and subsequent magical gifts in.

There are more Passages to go through, of course. Beyond the puberty rites, there are Handfastings, and Handpartings, if we need them; Queenings and Kingings; Cronings and Sagings; and Deathings and Requiems. There are Initiations and Elevations, too. As I hope and recommend that people be already raised and grown-up before they go through any of those other rites, though, they're not included in this book.

Our aim in raising our own son was, and is, to facilitate his becoming a caring and competent adult, and at 22, he's doing fine so far. We still cringe when we hear people say they wished their children could stay little forever. Eeewww! No, thanks! Yes, the little ones do tend to offer great photo opportunities, but our children "growing and going" doesn't empty our lives at all! No, no, the process is actually expansive. The way we see it, if the Explorer ever moves away from Tucson, sure, we'll miss him, but his place will be an auxiliary Great Hall, so to speak. It gives us a home in yet another place!

Having children is an awesome honor, and it comes with a lot of responsibility. Wiccan parents have an added responsibility, and that is to counter (early and often) the lies we know people are still telling about Neo-Pagan religions in general and Wicca in particular. This book is meant to be one tool for Wiccan parents to use in the deliberate education of their children—Wicca's future.

What's a Child Ready to Learn About Wicca?

Age	Developmental Needs/ Tasks/Challenges	Aspects of Wicca
Infancy	Trust that basic needs will be met	Chants for lullabies, movement to lively Pagan music, exposure to candles and incense
Early Childhood (1-5)	Separation and limits, security and routine place in family, control of body, development of speech	Learn to vent anger and frustration in simple rituals using physical energy, basic seasonal/ elemental correspondences, initial exposure to Craft etiquette, familiarity with and respect for Nature

Later Childhood (6-11)	Identity and independence, trust of adults other than parents, privacy, exploration of the world outside the home, reason and skepticism, trial and error, reassurance of worth	Explanation of secrecy, Directional and Tool associations and uses, chants, seasonal and Trad stories, some history and introduction to comparative religion, simple herb work
Adolescense (12-15)	Peer relationships, the future, the community, self-consciousness, emotional roller coaster, changes in body, increasing reponsibilities	Visualization, meditation, symbol and metaphor, more history, ethics, basic magic, calling Quarters or simple invocation, personal relationship with Goddess and God, personal use of magic and ritual, own altar, own Book of Shadows, comprehension of Rede and Law, introduction to group work
Young Adulthood (16+)	Transition to adulthood, control of emotional energy, widening perspective and use of experience to make choices, introspection, testing values and standards, internalized commitments	Initiation, own tools, full participation in ritual, coven membership, historical context, participation in groups and gatherings, divination, independent research

Infancy

Age
birth to 1 year old

Developmental Needs/Work/Challenges
Trust, basic needs met

Aspects of Wicca
Chants for lullabies, movement to lively Pagan music

We, that is our culture, used to think that babies couldn't see very well, couldn't learn or *know* anything. In the last few years, we have learned that it's not like that at all. Not only can babies see perfectly well until our medicines blur their vision, but they have innate expectations that the world is organized.

Experiments from as long ago as the 1980s showed that very young children respond with satisfaction to the appearance first of two dolls (each appearing alone) and then of the pair of them appearing together; they show distress when two single dolls are followed by one or three together. Basic math.

Babies also respond to the messages their mothers' facial expressions send in a fairly practical manner. If they encounter a new environment, they check to see if Mommy's smiling, and if she is, let the exploration begin; but if she looks anxious, yell for help. (The usual test is the raised Plexiglas floor, across which the infants hesitate to crawl, lest they fall; but if Mommy's smiling and encouraging on the other side, then baby takes a deep breath and heads out over the apparent abyss. That's pretty important reasoning and understanding and it's not a bad example of "perfect love, perfect trust," either.) Film of four-month-olds, shown at slow speed, reveals deliberate tracking and reaching behavior camouflaged by undeveloped motors skills. Children have expectations, and they start learning immediately; hence, whether consciously or not, parents start teaching immediately.

You might think that you can't "teach" an infant much about the Craft, but you might be wrong. You can't teach them the way you teach a college student, but with every breath, babies learn more about the world they've come into. Although they don't have the same sense of it that grown-ups do, babies have a very strong sense of time. They will establish schedules, even if the schedules are not the ones we parents like.

Most Witches find that it's helpful to set aside working time, whether for meditation, or magic, or some other Craft work. That's a regular time, the same time every day, the same day every week, the same night every month. Our mundane lives are full of routines, too, and we depend on them.

Babies have this reliance on routine in common with us. If you make it a point to daily take some Magical Time with your baby, the habit of setting aside time for magic will be well set. You will have to reinforce it by taking that time *with* your child for many years to come. This may be inconvenient sometimes, but not only will it be good for your child, it will be good for you as well!

How do you take Magical Time with a baby? Well, we must first acknowledge that *all* time with babies is magical. That said, a room lit with only one or two candles, a comfortable chair, and a mellow tape—deep, slow drumming, for instance (heartbeat drumming would be heavenly), or Enya played softly—makes a nice setting. What are some Magic Time activities? Well, you can rock and sing. You can enjoy an (herbal) sponge bath. You can give your baby a massage. You can get a big feather and some incense to waft around the room, trying a new one every week.

Can you teach babies as a group? Sure! Infants' swimming classes do (think about enrolling in one), and any community can bring babies together for communal magic and play times.

Remember that babies respond very well to bright colors and strong designs. (You may love those darling pastels, but they won't do much for your baby.) We used to fill the Explorer's room with exotic posters we'd find in small shops, some of them splashy and jewel-toned, some of them stark black and white. You can experiment with color and texture, finding or making posters that catch your child's attention.

Canyondancer and the Explorer drift together in a magical pre-sleep dance.

All of these activities help infants learn to love their body, develop their physical senses, and adjust to a variety of different environments. These activities will help babies identify certain perceptions and sensations with pleasure so that later, when they begin to learn about the religion of Wicca, the trappings will recall the love and trust of infancy.

(And if your children find a different religion when they grow up, the foundation of their childhood will support creativity and compassion in any religious context.)

What Babies Need Most

What children need most from us when they are babies is security. This translates into changing diapers as soon as they're wet or mucky, feeding on demand, and lots of snuggling, talking, singing, and touching. Sometimes, you hear that crying babies should be left alone, that they're just trying to manipulate you. Well, gosh, if they *can't* manipulate you, they'll *die*! They can't change their own diapers or get their own food; they can't defend themselves against the elements or saber-tooth tigers. They can't interpret anything or delay gratification the way we do. They even learn self-comforting behaviors from our interaction with them. We are their *only* security at first.

When the Explorer was a baby, he intensely disliked being alone at night. Our pediatrician advised us to let him cry himself out, that he "just wanted attention." It was physically agonizing for us to hear him, and we never could follow the doctor's instructions. Instead, though we lost sleep aplenty, we got up and went to him. Although we still say, "he didn't sleep through the night until he was 5," he has no doubt today that we are "here for him," as the saying goes. His need for comfort (trust and security) having been met, he's been able to move on.

Babies learn about the world primarily through their physical senses. The first thing they work on is basic coordination so they can get things into their mouths. The mouth is a very sensitive organ, and it does more than taste things. You can determine the size, texture, and at least some of the composition of a thing if you put it in your mouth. Sucking is not only a feeding behavior, it's also a comforting behavior (hence pacifiers). As babies's coordination improves, they'll start patting and stroking, again, for comfort.

Comfort and discomfort are the world to a baby. Crying signals discomfort. We can't always fix what's wrong but we *can* let our children know that they are loved and cared for no matter what. Putting babies away to fall tearfully into an exhausted sleep leaves them alone when they are desolate, and this makes a nasty imprint on their neural circuits. We want our children to know that no matter how gloomy it gets, they are never alone, and that we won't turn away just because we can't make it better.

Many of us are tempted to turn away when our friends have problems we can't make better. It makes us feel small, vulnerable, and helpless when there's nothing we can do. But if you go with that scared-little-inner-child feeling for a moment, you'll realize that "just being there" is doing something. It's being there. Going to the babies when they cry, even if you can't figure out why they're crying, even if holding and rocking doesn't make it stop, is doing something. It's caring, it's facing it together, it's loving the baby more than you love your own discomfort. Would you rather be hugged, or shut away when you're hurt or scared?

The concept of "the inner child" is well-known now, and it is through our inner child that we can commune with infants; for within all of us there is a babe with freshly powdered bottom, wriggling in delight to be warm and dry and gazing into Mother's face. The physical basics that would comfort you will probably comfort your baby. When all else fails, find a comfortable chair and bounce or rock and hug and sing. If your baby keeps crying, sing to your own inner child. (If that fails in the middle of the night, take a deep breath, ground and center, and turn on the lights. Play daytime for a few minutes and then try bedtime again.)

Touching Auras

When the Explorer was little, I was often able to help him through a rough spot in his sleep by projecting calm energy to his aura, even through his bedroom door. Can you see your baby's aura? Can you see your own? You can practice in front of the bathroom or bedroom mirror when your baby is calm, but in the meantime....

Whether or not you can see auras, you can visualize yours touching your baby's, infusing it with trust, comfort, and security. If your baby is agitated, send a mellowing blue into her aura. Focus on your breathing to give her a calm anchor.

In addition to helping your baby calm down, you'll also be showing him that moods and feelings *are* under our control, an important concept for all of us to internalize. This may take some practice, but the quiet time and concentration you spend with your baby will strengthen the bond between you, no matter what your results are.

Remember that babies are not using their left brains very often. They cannot "listen to reason." They respond to your expressions, your tone, even your aura; but they do not think as we do. As adults, we're the ones with the capacity to reason, the capacity to differentiate between ourselves and our environments, and the capability of meeting needs. We must meet our infants' needs carefully so that they do not become permanently dependent upon us or anyone else.

Babies need to be empowered. They need to be loved unconditionally, and be safe as they experiment with their environment. They need to experience and internalize certainty and trust. They need to be held when they cry, changed when they're wet, and fed when they're hungry, even if they don't keep our schedules. Babies are in transition between the "Whole" environment of the womb and the "Individual" world out here. We need to be gentle with them, as gentle as we'd want people to be with us.

This, however, is not to say you shouldn't aim for getting the child on a sleeping and eating schedule that your household can live with, only that you shouldn't "force it down his throat." When the children wake up in the middle of the night and howl for you, it's because they think they need you, and whether you or the doctor thinks they need you or not is completely meaningless. What matters is whether babies can count on you to respond to them when they are in distress.

We were all infants once, of course. Just as our babies are completely dependent on us for all their needs, so were we dependent on someone else to meet our needs when we were babies. If our needs *weren't* met, then we might not have a very good idea of how to nurture our own or other people's children. This is, of course, not our fault; but with an infant to take care of, it might be a problem.

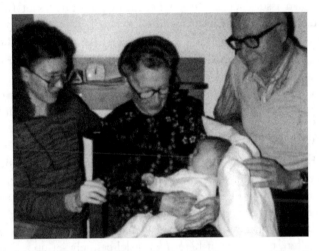

Three generations are on hand to nurture and pass along skills and interests to the infant Explorer.

You can know how you *don't* want to interact with children without knowing exactly how you *do* want to relate. You might have heard yelling often enough to understand that it's horrible and not what you want to do, and still not know what it looks like to do anything else. But you can find out, and practice until it comes just as naturally as yelling used to. (Yes, I am speaking from experience.) Sometimes it takes long-term interaction with children to show you that some of your own "child needs" are unmet.

Well, as the T-shirt says, "It's never too late to have a happy childhood." We recommend John Bradshaw's *Homecoming: Reclaiming and Championing Your Wounded Inner Child.* (There is also a set of lectures, originally presented on PBS, available on videotape.)

If parenting or teaching at any stage brings up unresolved issues from your own childhood, show yourself the same respect you'd show to anyone else, and *deal* with those issues. There are many books out there, and there are counselors and groups (covered by insurance or on sliding scales) in a lot of places, not just major metropolitan areas. You'll be more effective and have more fun if you can come to teach Wicca with your own issues settled, not ignored, not devalued, not ridiculed, not postponed, not disowned.

Most of us are working with the idea that "what we went through in our childhood" has strengthened us. The late Carlos Castaneda's teacher, Don Juan, praises the usage of petty tyrants, and Brooke Medicine Eagle can call a man who abused her a teacher. Some of us remember being told that disappointment, pain, fear, and abuse are "good for our character."

Well, making lemonade out of lemons is one thing, but it's not bad for anybody to get the orange juice or apple juice they really wanted. Babies are naturally trusting, and only nurturing that trust will give them the strength they need to weather the world. Making infancy harsh is *not* preparation for the real worlds. It's abusive, unnecessary, and *very* bad magic. We don't say "never" very often, but we say it here: *Never* deliberately set up a child to teach him or her how harsh the world is.

Babies respond well to things that stimulate their senses: color, sound, smell, and texture. Most of us are familiar with the "baby monkey" studies demonstrating babies' critical need for holding and stroking. Fill your children's lives with these elements, and they'll be on the way to a healthy Wiccan adulthood.

As long as you stay in the room, you can burn candles in the nursery. They make a much nicer light than incandescents or (ugh) fluorescent lights, and in the winter, they add a little warmth. (If you want to burn a candle even in the summer, when you have to run a fan or air conditioning, then just put a glass chimney around the candle.)

Although we can't really know what's going on in their minds, we know that babies have longer attention spans than once thought, and candle flames fascinate them. Get them started early on candle gazing! Sing them stories of what *you* see in the flames. They will always be comfortable with candles if you make this small effort to predispose them.

Incense: Absent serious allergy problems, they'll enjoy it. (Start with delicate scents; and if your baby doesn't like it, get rid of it.) The smoke can be neat to watch. The smells stimulate babies, and can get them accustomed to the scents you use most often. This will start building important associations. Smell is the most evocative of our senses—who hasn't been taken right back to a certain time and place, or mood, by a smell? If your babies learn to associate incense (and candles) with comfort, love, and trust, they will be able to build on that foundation later.

Fire and Air Blessing

Select a new candle in an energetic color; 6-inch drip tapers are nicely proportioned for babies' rooms. Select your favorite sort of incense—stick, cone, or powder—in what you consider an Easterly scent.

Clear space for an Altar—temporary, if need be—in the Southeast. (East represents beginnings, South is growth and strength. Placing the Altar in the Southeast will make it a psychic beacon to mark the direction in which your baby is proceeding around the Wheel.)

Preferably with your baby's attention (it's alright if the baby's sleeping, but baby does need to be in the room when you do this), light the incense, and fanning some over the baby, say,

> Breath of Life, Spirit of East,
>
> bless this child in faith and feast.
>
> Keep her sight with wonder filled;
>
> let fears by power of mind be stilled.

Light the candle and say,

> Flame of Spirit, Heart of South,
>
> bless this child with a passionate youth.
>
> By power of Son and Lover both,
>
> call her ever on to growth.

Focus on the flame and project its energy into your baby's aura. Let both incense and candle burn as long as you can stay in the room with the baby. (You don't have to be quiet, either; sing and cuddle and gurgle all you want. Those are blessings, too.)

I've mentioned color as an important influence on infants, and we all know that colors can stimulate us or calm us down. Mundanely, we have all kinds of color associations—from holidays to sports teams. Color has strong psychological and physical effects on us...so how do we introduce our children to the power of colors?

Well, there are the walls of Baby's room, though we don't recommend painting more than one or two walls of any room in bright colors. (We do, however, recommend letting children choose the colors they want in their rooms as soon as they have preferences. You don't like it? It's not your room! It's only paint, and even a marble wall veined with gold isn't more important than your children and their childhood memories.) A design or mural covering the whole area or a border around the baseboards or near the ceiling is always nice. There are wallpaper strips in a variety of designs, and you can buy stencils or make them yourself.

You can hang bright posters on the walls, and you can use color in your window coverings as well. You can even substitute curtains for doors. You can use color (and design) in floor covering: there are carpets made with game-board designs and roadlike stripes and swirls, or you can paint the floor or arrange tile or paint a canvas floor cloth.

And don't forget Baby's wardrobe! Socially, clothing colors indicate the gender of a baby (and there've been some amusing studies done about the way people treat babies depending on the colors they're wearing). In our Pagan culture, colors mean a good deal more.

We know that color can have tremendous effect. The traditional-for-infants pastels are sort of enervating, while bright colors are stimulating. Interesting, isn't it, that many baby clothes, most schools, and most prisons all tend to be done in pale shades, while shopping malls, commercials and cars are all bright. Society is pretty clear about when we should be passive and when we should be active!

Right through later childhood, the Explorer enjoyed eclectic posters, one red wall, stars and stripes curtains, and strands of colored lights brightening his room.

Pagans are equally clear. We like vibrant colors, and we're inclined to use them—and to wear them—medicinally as well as according to their religious significance. We like fiery red during the Winter, when we need to be encouraged. We like yellow in the Spring; we like blue and green when we're over-excited, orange when we need more energy.

Well, babies need the same things. We need to remember that society's ideas of "gender-appropriate" colors might not accommodate psycho-magical associations of mood-appropriate colors. We can guide our children early into self-confidence if we guide them with color.

Color Rhyme

> Red is for life, orange for balance
> Yellow's for thought and developing talents
> Green is for nature and blue is for spirit
> Indigo's peace: be quiet to hear it.
> Violet's primal, enchanted and fine:
> They make up the rainbow, and you make it shine.

Sound is important, too. Hum, click, talk, sing, chant—your baby can *feel* you sing as well as hear you. Experiment with keys and tones until you find the vibrations that you and your baby like best, and then work with them. (Babies feel good about repetition.) This is the best time to introduce your baby to chants—if you have tapes, play them; if you don't, sing. Use chants familiar to you from Circle, but vary the words as you're moved to.

Rhythm is important to infants. It's a link between this new "outside world" and the womb. They like beats that are in heart-beat range, of course. This is a great time to let them listen—and wiggle and giggle—to a variety of percussion. There are lots of tapes available, featuring various cultures' drumming. (Some have vocal backgrounds.)

You'll soon learn which music your baby likes best. There are still Gordon Lightfoot, Linda Ronstadt, and Eagles albums *we* can't hear without crooking elbows and starting to sway, still rocking the baby to sleep years after he's grown up, because we played them at least twice every night when the Explorer was a baby. (It was nice, going into light trance with him like that. And it's a pleasant "flash back" now when we hear that music.)

Dance with babies! You don't have to be able to carry Baby around to dance, either. I remember the Explorer laying on his back on the living room floor, me on my knees leaning over him. He'd hold one of my fingers in each of his tiny hands, and I'd dance his arms to all kinds of music. Then we'd dance his "toesies," too. Later, when he was beginning to stand and bounce, we'd *bounce* to all kinds of music. Daddy danced with him too—it was great fun for all of us!

Environmental tapes are readily available now, so take advantage of this. If you live where there are lots of thunderstorms, for instance, get a tape of rain and thunder and play it when your baby's young, so that there's an association of comfort, rather than fear, with those sounds. Any natural sounds will soothe your baby—loons on a lake, fire crackling, rain falling, birds singing.

If there are environmental sounds that *you* associate with fear, get tapes of those. You'll be surprised how easily you can recondition yourself if you play those tapes while you're hold-ing and rocking your baby. Babies can't say much and they aren't really well-coordinated at first, but they sure can heal. However, if there's something you're so scared of that your vibes agitate the baby, then leave it alone while you're with the baby, and work through it on your own.

Make a tape recording of yourself singing to your baby! Fill a whole cassette with it, maybe not all at one sitting. It'll be available whenever you're not, and you might be surprised to find that your child will enjoy it for many years. We are often our least inhibited with babies, and there is a quality of "ego-less-ness" in a parent's singing to a child. (For instance, "it's Mommy potty time" to the tune of "ta ra ra boom de ay.") Children need us to be ego-less quite often, for a long time.

We made some audio tapes when the Explorer was growing up, and they delight us to this day. There are qualities of "ego-less-ness" in children's explanations of what they see and conclude, too, and it is strangely reassuring as well. Some of these precious conversa-tions were with the Explorer before he was articulate, and they're wonderful. When we listen to them together, the three of us expe-rience that pre-verbal state—we laugh so hard we cry and can't speak! The sound of children's laughter is one of the best sounds the planet has to offer—and it *is* an offering. Her worship, the Charge tells us, is in the heart that rejoices.

It is unquestionably boggling to look at an infant and *know* that this small baby-thing will mature and be like you (sort of). Able to reach things and think and be in touch with its feelings. Someday, the baby-thing you gaze upon will be standing as you are standing, gazing upon another baby-thing, feeling the same sense of awe in the face of Mystery. It can be overwhelming and sometimes a care-taking adult needs a little support, too.

Charm for Caring Grown-Ups

For this you will need a piece of the baby's birthstone, some water or oil (baby oil is fine), and a piece of cloth with some ribbon or a pouch you've made yourself. As you say the third line, anoint the birthstone, hold it to your heart, and then raise it to your lips to breathe on it. When you're done, wrap the stone in the cloth or pouch, and tuck it somewhere close to you.

> East and South and West and North
> Bless this life that love brought forth,
> By stone and drop and spark and gust,
> May I ever support her trust.
> Lady of the Cauldron, Lord of the Lance,
> Help me to teach her the steps to the Dance.

Most of us don't feel awe very often in our "regular" lives. Why, we're hardly surprised by anything any more. We're almost jaded, close to cynical. And then we look at a baby, and we discover that we can still be moved. The joy an infant can generate touches the potential joy of the infant within, and the thrill is so unfamiliar to so many of us now that we sometimes pull away from it. Don't.

It may overwhelm you. You may weep. It's okay. Plunge into that joy, into the Mystery, into the trust and love. (It's pretty common to experience a three-day "high" after attending a birth. Everybody cries and hugs and you see the world more gently for the next few days, without even trying.) Immerse yourself, wallow, and luxuriate.

That's what it's there for. This is very close to integration of wholeness with individuality: through that baby's undifferentiated being, you can be both parent and child, whole and individual. It is a precious opportunity, and it comes from the Source of all consciousness, and it's wonderful to have that perspective again.

"In the best of times, our days are numbered anyway. And so it would be a crime against nature for any generation to take the world crisis so solemnly that it puts off enjoying those things for which we were presumably designed in the first place...the opportunity to do good work, to fall in love, to enjoy friends, to hit a ball, and to bounce a baby." Alistair Cooke said that in *One Man's America* (1952), and we copied it into the Explorer's baby album; and we're copying it here, too, because we think it's worth repeating.

There are lots of reasons not to have a baby, and they all come down to one thing: fear. Fear that you'll be a bad parent. Fear that something will be wrong with the baby. Fear the child will grow up only to turn bad. And it's true; lots of things can go wrong. One of the Explorer's high school memories is of the death of a 15-year-old boy who lived across the street from us, his drive-by shooter never caught. So he wonders how good it would be to bring a child into the world: What if the baby grows up and gets shot too?

Hard question; but if you ask the parents of that 15-year-old, I'll bet they don't say they wish their son had never been born, that they'd never had those 15 years with him. Ultimately, the fact that things change and people die is no excuse. (Ultimately, the fact that things change and people die—and are reborn—is the fact we honor in our worship!) Something horrifies every generation, yet there's always another one. The effort is always worth it, and facing fears is always an opportunity for growth.

When people try to avoid the hurts of life by shutting down their feelings, they find that they avoid all the joys as well. Life is depressing and unsatisfying—not because other people are making it their life's work to thwart you, but because you won't take the risk of pain for joy. (Where there's fear there can be no love; where there's love there can be no fear. Those are the words of one of Wicca's chants, and though they exaggerate a bit, they make the point.) Life is not set up so that we have to suffer pain equal to every joy, but lots of people think so, and they think the way not to feel pain is to bar joy. Nope. It's the decision to sacrifice joy that causes pain. Babies are joy. All they ask in return is the occasional clean diaper and your acceptance of their joy. This is, for us, a much smaller risk than the one they take by being born.

Here's a lullaby I wrote for a character in an unpublished sci-fi novel to sing to her children, and then to her story-companions. It's even more special to us now, for we presently have, in the coven, a 4-year-old by the same name.

Ivy's Song

Green and blue and black and white
Planet Earth and Mother Night
Home to body, jewel to sight
Round, round; round around, round around
Round, round; round around, round around

Red and yellow, Earth and Air
Fur and feather, fin and hair
All so common, all so rare
Round, round; round around, round around
Round, round; round around, round around

Gold and silver, fire and rain
Birth and death, joy and pain
Breath and heartbeat, wax and wane
Round, round; round around, round around
Round, round; round around, round around

Man and woman, spirits, heart
Change in science, grow in art
Never finish, always start
Round, round; round around, round around
Round, round; round around, round around

Early Childhood

Age

1 year old to 5 years old

Developmental Tasks/ Work/ Challenges

Separation and limits, security and routine, place in family, basic control of body, speech development

Aspects of Wicca

Learn to vent anger, frustration in simple rituals using physical energy; exposure to Craft etiquette, familiarity with and respect for Nature; seasonal/elemental correspondences

Aren't children between the ages of 1 and 5 great? They've got their incarnation legs by now, mostly, and they're heading out for the first time. They have to learn *everything*! From the layout of the house to this *talking* thing, everything is a lot. It is this enormous task they need to accomplish in a mere five years that requires them to have their prodigious energy.

Just as you can overfill the chalice with the wine, children's energy can become too fast for even a Witch to handle, so you don't have to feel guilty if you lose it sometimes. If you find yourself using physical discipline frequently and then feeling lousy about it, you don't have to shame yourself into isolation and denial. You *do* need to get some help with anger management, find somebody to help out with whatever isn't getting done, or otherwise get away from physically disciplining the child a lot, because hitting people is wrong; but shame and guilt won't offer you any help or growth. (By the way, I mention this not because Pagan parents are angry parents, but because even one child's life is more important than anybody who gets snippy about having to hear it.)

Needing to learn is not a moral flaw. We've met a lot of parents who have little children who need that reassurance. Apart from your personal experience, which may not contain useful examples of positive parenting, there are the social images: *Leave it to Beaver* and *The Brady Bunch* contrast with "reality," and the media show us child abuse and molestation in every edition. So the wonder is how we do as well as we do. That all of us could use a little advice about the children sometimes is just a fact, not a judgment.

Priestess-mommy Chandra Nelson sways and sings to toddler Ivy, who can't run around, as they wait thir turn to put left-over Yule greenery on the Bride Fire.

Needing to learn is not a moral flaw. We've met plenty of little children who need that reassurance, too. Apart from their personal experience, which may not include any examples of guiltless learning, there are the social images: a brother or sister that they can't be enough like; or gangs, murder, and drugs with every rising of the sun. So the wonder is how children survive as well as they do. Sometimes all of us could use a little advice about growing up.

Don't the young children you know get angry sometimes? Of course they do! Chances are that they can't really tell you about it, though. Fact is, they can't understand it very well, either. Children don't have much experience to guide their interpretations and decisions, and their capacity to reason won't be fully developed for years. You can't always talk them out of their anger. If they're young enough, you can distract them, but if you keep that up, you give them the impression their feelings don't count. If you deny their anger, or any other feelings, they will come to doubt you or themselves. It's a good idea to recognize young children's anger and show them ways to vent and ground it. There's no need to condemn it—anger has its place in our emotions. Anger used to move us mostly to violence, and still moves us in self-defense or in the aid of others. But modern Witches have many other ways of venting and spinning that energy.

Have children draw a picture of how angry they are. Provide crayons, chalk, or finger-paints—anything that doesn't hurt to push hard. Chalk and crayons may break, but they won't explode or slice your child's finger off, and they'll still *work* when they're broken. For paper, use anything from stationery to a cut-open grocery bag. When all the anger is projected into the artwork, ask the children how they think they might get rid of it.

If children suggest an impractical disposition, such as flushing a large piece of construction paper down the toilet, come as close as you can. Let them smoosh their art completely under water in a spaghetti pan, or a toy swimming pool, maybe scrubbing the image off.

Young Children's Anger

It is generally best to involve young children in some *physical* grounding of their anger. Most grown-ups long for a run on the beach, or want to pound something when we get mad, but we know lots of non-physical ways to get rid of anger for those times when we *can't* run and pound. For children, there are no non-physical ways.

It's up to us to provide them with safe physical outlets for their feelings so they can learn to "own" their feelings and take responsibility for them, without being intimidated or over-whelmed. Hitting pillows is okay, but we need to emphasize that hitting people, or animals, or plants is *not* okay. "I feel angry when ——," are the words of effective anger. "You make me mad" is not effective.

When children are young, the way they can "take responsi-bility" for their feelings is by getting familiar with them. As their teachers, we must work really hard not to *shame* our chil-dren for their feelings, even though we might have been shamed (or smacked) for ours.

One way to deal with anger, akin to hitting pillows but more dramatic, is to stomp it out. Put sand or dirt or even a pile of dirty laundry down so the child can jump up and down on it until the pile is flattened and the anger is exhausted. The energy goes into the ground, the children see that they've *done* something, and with that energy vented, children feel better. We have to teach our children that it's okay to *feel* anger (and everything else), but there are only certain ways we can *express* it (or any other feeling). Look for opportunities to talk to your children about their feel-ings and appropriate ways to express feelings before they get out of control.

If you live where you can allow screaming without alarming the neighbors, so much the better. If the children are at the "**NO**" stage, then a vigorous chant of *Nah! Nah! Nah!* moving into *Ah! Ah! Ah!* and finally into an affirmative *Yah! Yah! Yah!*—if carefully guided by an attentive parent-priestess or -priest—can do wonders to change a mood. Music can work, too—find some that starts out energetically and then calms down, and show your children how to dance from anger to calmness. Entering an anger-grounding process into a child's motor memory means it'll be available to him all his life.

Mythical Children

Between the ages of 1 and 5, children are relatively mythical, which is to say, they like the sort of rituals and important things that happen in fairy tales. They are naturally dramatic, and predisposed to the sort of medieval manners that Witches enjoy. This is, of course, wonderful.

A lot of little children—sometimes until they're nearly adolescent—have imaginary friends. (Mine was a beautiful buckskin stallion I called Salishan.) Unless they keep children from human friendships, or inspire them to self-destructive behavior, imaginary friends are fine. Salishan went to pasture when I was about 11 years old, but now and again he pokes his head in to remind me that I can still enjoy the wind in my hair. Your child might have an imaginary playmate too. Be respectful, because that imaginary friend is helping your kid sort out myriad questions about identity and limits.

Little children, usually because we tell them to, also believe in characters such as the Sandman, the Ostara bunny, the Tooth Fairy, and Santa Claus. What about them? At some point, we all realize they aren't discrete individuals like we are. Does that mean they're not real?

Are you familiar with the distinction psychology makes between the personal unconscious and the collective unconscious? Imaginary friends are aspects of our personal unconscious, while Santa and the rest of that lot are aspects of our collective unconscious. What manifests through our collective unconscious is what is most real to humanity.

Santa Claus is comin' to town...isn't he?

One way we can explain this to children is through analogy. Let's use love as an example. Love is part of your child's experience, but it isn't an object, like a tree or a car; or a one-right-answer thing like math; and we can't measure it like we do distance or weight. We know it's real, though, because we can feel its effects. Love has lots of effects, too: Mommy's and Daddy's kisses, Grammy's and Grampy's hugs and phone calls, friends' smiles—and how many more? Love is so real, it needs lots of ways to express itself. Santa and the Tooth Fairy, the Ostara bunny and the Sandman are all aspects of the love of the God or Goddess for us and the rest of life, and yes, they're real.

There are, as Wiccans know and profess, many sorts of reality. In practical terms, children need practice with the down-to-earth sort before they're ready to cope with alternates. As soon as a young children is ready, give them a compass; that way they can always find North, which is an important skill materially and symbolically. Properly presented, it can be clear to children that a compass is a Magical Tool, a special gift. Put it in a pouch!

While we're on the subject of finding North, and how important that is symbolically, let's not forget to introduce our children to correspondences. Young children are ready to learn about "go-togethers." Make some simple associations for them—colors and shapes, things they're already learning. Listen to their correspondence suggestions, encourage them if they're getting it right (per your sensibilities and Tradition) and steer them right if they're getting lost.

For an on-going lesson in correspondences, quarter a large circle (drawn on poster board, maybe). Label each quarter with a season, and over time, fill that space with appropriate pictures, cut from magazines or drawn by hand. Take a whole year to finish it, and you'll help develop your child's sense of time, and the idea that life works in cycles, and....

The-old fashioned Nature walk is an excellent teaching tool, and long walks help children (and grown-ups) sleep well at night, too. If you don't know about the things that grow in your area, go to the library and find out. Check to see if there are parks that attract certain wildlife, or parks that have marked Nature walks.

The first time the Explorer found out for himself that ponderosa pine bark smells like vanilla, he was astonished. We like to see that wide-eyed look in children. It means magic has

Children can explore correspondences as they add their finds to
Altars like this. Carved jack-o'-lanterns flank this one,
built on a campground table.

touched them. The first glow-worms you see, the first cicada shell, the first snakeskin are all little gifts from Mother Nature, and are all bases for lessons, too.

If you're excited about the neat things children find on the ground in the forest, their excitement will be lasting, too. If you cherish the experiences you have in "the woods," so will they. There's an alarming number of Pagans who don't like the out-of-doors and have never circled anywhere wilder than their backyards, if they've circled outside at all. I think that's a loss to our souls, not to mention bad news for an environment that needs as much love and care as it can get. And if you show your young students how to look for the small and hidden wonders in the regular world, they'll have that skill and comfort forever.

Sometimes young children tell us stories. The child of some Witches here in Tucson grew up telling his mom stories about "when I was big," and she listened carefully and made notes, because those might have been memories of past lives. Children tell stories of doings in dimensions we can't see, too. If you see a child who is a budding storyteller, encourage him! Tape the stories. Ask for illustrations. Encourage children to act out the stories as they tell them, using stuffed animals and dolls or costumes, even rudimentary or minimalist sets, when those are appropriate. Get out the camera!

If your child likes the idea, you can even make dolls of friends met in other experiences. (You can make a set of play poppets from round-head clothes pins and circles of cloth. We try to make a clothespin doll or two, and at least one pouch, out of scraps of every robe and costume we make. You could do something similar with wrapping paper. Dolls like these can be the cast of "story-spells," too.)

If you've ever noticed children at play, you'll have seen that they act out vignettes symbolizing situations they anticipate facing, practicing the social tools they'll be expected to use. Story-spells do so consciously, from a total suspension of disbelief; it's a kind of lucid dreaming. As mundane play-figures enjoy some superhuman powers but are still bound by other rules of their lands or stories, so our poppets may fly or have other "powers," but they're still bound by Wiccan ethics.

From apparently ordinary play to story-spells is barely a step for young children. But play itself is difficult for some adults, and story-spells can help redevelop our ability to be playful. There is something about a doll or puppet that helps us suspend our disbelief, almost like going to a movie. So while we're introducing our children to magic and ethics through the use of story-spells, we can also be reintroducing ourselves to kinds of magic we may not have worked since childhood.

Story-spells may be more commonly used than most of us realize. We know that many athletes "visualize" successful strokes or dunks, and focus on winning. If an athlete, or a student, or an executive imagines the whole game or test or presentation, any practical line between "visualization" and "story-spell" blurs.

Story-Spells

The reality of fiction and the power of "the word," of language, of spell-casting and story-telling, is recognized in every faith and culture. Here's an example of a practical story-spell. Act it out with poppets or with twigs you find around the woods, or with actual persons.

> Once upon a time before there was time, three Princesses who were friends were taking a walk. They were stepping right along, really enjoying the scenery, when all of a sudden...they came to a tree fallen across their path!
>
> Well, now, the first Princess wanted to climb over. "Come on," she said, starting to scramble up.
>
> But, "Wait just a minute!" said one of the other Princeesses. "I think we should go around. You come on!"
>
> But then, "Wait another minute," said the third Princeess. "I think we should turn back. You come on!"
>
> For a very long time, they could not agree. They argued and argued. They got mad and stomped a little way off, and then came back and sat down.
>
> Then it started to snow! The three Princesses decided that getting by the fallen tree was more important than anybody being more right or more in charge than anyone else.
>
> And then, without arguing or even thinking about it, they all three got up and pushed the fallen tree out of their way, and hurried on to the next castle to get out of the storm.

Young children are very literal-minded. Stick pretty close to their experience in these story-spells. Don't offer them figurative trees; they don't understand "figurative." Give them something relevant such as physical obstacles or how tempting that kitty's tail is. Make the characters royal and give them names the children recognize. Help them keep the story focused on really possible resolutions. If the ideas of the Princesses (or Princes) get too off the wall, they must be reminded there are rules that even royalty must follow; keep limitations in the character.

Some stories go beyond this, though, being shared with us by the "Little People living in the tales we tell," as we said in *The Family Wicca Book*. Story *blessings* are stories that tell themselves to us; encourage this delightful sort of channeling in children who are open to it. Encourage it in yourself, too.

When we are trying to teach children to follow certain rules, it's helpful if we obey them as well. If we want children to learn to cut a door before entering or leaving a Circle, and not to touch things on altars, then we must take care, always, to knock before we enter their rooms, to ask before we pick up their things, and to speak as though we value those protocols. (The idea of asking our children's permission, and respecting our children's denials as well as their acquiescence, is alarming to some people and downright offensive to others. As far as we're concerned, however, it's a cornerstone of Wiccan parenting, and we'll talk more about it later.)

Once children have a basic understanding of altar space, (which generally happens around the age of 3, when ideas of territory begin to occur), they may want to set up a personal altar. This is great! If there is any community space (maybe in that little corner of the yard) that can facilitate children's Circles, several children's altars standing around it would be charming (literally and figuratively). Friends of ours did this, and the cock-eyed Circle with its innocent offerings was preciously refreshing.

In your sewing or craft room or at a thrift shop, you can find rugs, or place mats, or doilies—even small tables—to serve as altars and cloths. The Explorer's first altar was set up on a geometrically patterned rug he found at Value Village. Each time he set it up, he chose where to put the white ceramic Buddha and Kwan Yin he used. Sometimes the Explorer put other things on his altar, according to his intuition at the time; and if one of us was with him, he could light a candle. Later, when there was less space in his room for a personal altar, the permanent altar outside made sense to him. He learned early, too, how to arrange the more intricate indoor Altar we use in most coven rituals.

Having the opportunity in early childhood to experiment with altar-building, the children we teach may approach the

Using decades-old clothespin dolls, sisters Caitlin
and Rowan plan out a story-spell.

task almost instinctively as adults. We consider this to be resto-
ration, not a new development for humans. Learning about place-
ment on our altars also teaches our children, unconsciously at
first, something about how we organize our lives and priorities,
and it's their first introduction to Wicca's cosmology, too.

Experimenting with altar-building, is something grown-ups
can enjoy just as much as children do. At camp, the mood has
been just right to inspire us several times, and in the boles of
trees or on the ends of the Forest Service's cement tables, we've
set up rocks and sprigs and twigs and things we'd brought from
home (See photo on pg. 59). It doesn't happen every time, so
every time it does happen is palpably magical.

More and more often, still-broom-closeted Pagans and *non*-
Pagans are keeping Ancestor altars in their homes, too. Ranging from pictures of great-grandparents flanked by candles to
collections of family memorabilia, these New Age displays express a reverence not just for the individual lives they're dedicated to, but also for the cycle of life. Be alert to these set-ups so
you can point them out to your children and students.

Sometimes, altars (broadly defined as where we set out the symbols of our faith or belief) occur naturally, and require only the right vision to see them clearly. One Beltane when we were camped in New Mexico for the five days, one of the children, not quite 4 years old, pointed to a small flowering tree a few hundred yards away. "Let's go look at that Spring," she suggested winsomely. A blooming tree personified Spring for her; may it do as much for the rest of us! Not a conventional Altar at all, but through her eyes—thanks, love—we could see it as a living altar, perfectly expressing our faith and belief.

Following is another song, this one without any music—yet. That's because you, or your children, or all of you together, need to make up a tune of your own. You'll have no trouble at all coming up with one; using a tune you already know is fine. You can use the verses separately, and you can change the words when you arrange your altar differently. Better still, make up your own song for your own altar!

Up on the Altar

Up on the altar, what do I see?
I see candles, one, two three!
One for the Lady, one for the Lord,
And in the middle for little ol' me!

Up on the altar, what do I hear?
I hear the bell that rings so clear!
Once for the Lady, once for the Lord,
And one more time to call me near!

Up on the altar, what have I found?
I found a Pentagram, flat and round!
It's for the Lady and it's for the Lord,
And it's to help me center and ground!

Up on the altar, smooth and bright,
The altar-cloth glows in quiet light

Left for the Lady, right for the Lord
When I touch the altar-cloth it feels just right.

Up on the altar, what do I smell?
I smell the incense, starting to swell!
Some for the Lady, some for the Lord
And some for me 'cause I like it so well!

Up on the altar, what can I taste?
Cakes and ale that the Gods have graced!
Some for the Lady, some for the Lord,
And I get to share when it comes by my place!

A long, low Altar—his one in a small backyard—is easy for children to see and reach. (The kitty's name is Gracie.)

Up on the altar, what have we got?
We've got some tools we use a lot!
Some for the Lady, some for the Lord,
And some for me when I am taught!

Up on the altar, what can they be?
Figures standing sym-bol-ic-ly!
One is the Lady, one is the Lord,
And I know for sure that They love me!

When we're working with children, there is an occasional
need to stop or correct their behavior. Sometimes children do
things wrong—incorrectly—in which case they can be encouraged to try different approaches, without being particularly rep-
rimanded. Sometimes children do wrong things, and then they
must be first interrupted, and then advised that such behavior
is unacceptable.

Not too long ago, this conversation was overheard on a
city bus:

First Mom (in her 20s): "My daughter bites." (Her daughter is 2-ish.)
Second Mom (in her 40s): "They all bite."
Third Mom (in her 50s): "Yeah."
First Mom: "I've tried everything. I've taped her mouth, I've slapped her,
I've spanked her, I've sent her to her room. I don't know what else to do."
Second and Third Mom in unison: "Bite her back."

Oh, gosh, that is *so* wrong, that is just so, so wrong! All of
these efforts to change the child's behavior are shaming, and just
plain mean. And clearly none of them are effective. When the
infant Explorer tried biting, once, he heard a sharp and sudden
"No!" and found his mouth held shut for a few seconds. No pre-
tense of injury or guilt-tripping wails of pain, no anger, no long,
scary shouting. Just an unpleasant but nonjudgmental consequence.
He never bit anyone again.

Before we go any farther here, let's go back to that bus-
conversation for a minute. The first mom had done lots of things

to her child that adults will not tolerate. She taped the child's mouth—and in the news a few months after September 11, 2001 there were opinions voiced that gagging detainees constituted torture. The mom slapped her little girl. We all have our own opinions about the propriety of hitting a child, but the fact is that children who are hit quite often turn out to be hitters themselves. And, quite frankly, if another adult slapped us the way some people slap their children, we'd bring it to court as an assault case. Mom spanked the child, too—more hitting. Hitting rarely works unless you're trying to raise a bully.

Finally, this mother banished her child. (Maybe the child experienced it as a relief, though—at least Mom's not taping or hitting!) We think all this is awful, and for Wiccans, an abdication of faith. We believe that at least in our personal relationships, we can accomplish what we need to without using violence, and we think that resorting to violence of any kind is a mistake. A big one. Perhaps the violence represents an issue, maybe one that's been avoided for more than one lifetime.

Some parents use "time-outs" effectively. As we understand it, this method of correction involves isolating a child immediately after they've done something unacceptable, safely but without access to toys, and for no longer than a minute per year of the child's age. The idea is not for the children to "think about what they've done wrong," but to understand that certain behaviors put you outside the realm of human interaction. Children young enough to use "time-outs" on are too young to "think about what they did."

Think about how you want to be corrected when you make a mistake. Do you want to be hit? How about verbally abused? Do you want to be sent away in shame and fear without quite knowing what you did wrong or how you could correct your behavior? And when there are explanations, do you like it when they're in terms you don't understand? The answer to all those questions is probably "no."

If you offered these questions to children, they'd say "no" too. You can't control everything that happens to you, or to your child. You *can* control how you happen in the world. You won't teach your child self-control without demonstrating your own; and you won't honor the God and Goddess by forgetting how precious your children are, even when your head is pounding.

Canyondancer and I received advice from our own parents about teaching the Explorer, when he was learning to walk, to stop at corners. Sometimes, careening down the sidewalk, he'd get a few yards ahead, and we wanted him to make the habit of stopping at the curb, of not going into the street without someone. My parents encouraged spanking. We chose to parent differently.

There was virtually no daytime traffic where we lived, so it was safe to modify his behavior this way. The first time, we told him to stop at the curb, and he didn't. He got several steps into the street before he stopped. So we picked him up and said we were sorry he didn't stop at the curb and that we'd have to go back now. There were tears, but back we went.

We were perfectly pleasant and matter-of-fact about it. The second time, he hesitated at the curb and put one foot in the street, clearly testing the "asphalts." Well, that was just too bad. We had to go back. After that, having figured out the limits of acceptable behavior, he stopped at the curb without fail. Over the next few years, of course, we kept an eye out, unnoticed, and happily observed the Explorer stopping at the curb and checking for traffic before going into the street after a ball or a remote-controlled car. The children in our neighborhood who used to get smacked for dashing into the street when they were young kept right on dashing well into their teens!

When you have to discipline children—discipline means "teach," by the way, not "punish"—do so with the Rede and the Law in mind. Contrary to popular attitudes, children are not miniature adults. Nor are they chattel. They are human beings, living creatures, part of the Earth, and we harm them when we treat them otherwise.

Children do not misbehave to be bad; they don't, as a rule, plot to embarrass or inconvenience us. They do what gives them power and identity. Are they going about it the wrong way? Then our job is to show them a right way. If only their "bad" behavior gets noticed, then only their "bad" behavior is encouraged, so naturally, they pursue it; they'll take what they can get. That's their survival instinct at work. Rewarded with positive attention when their behavior is appropriate, they'll understand that you seek power through cooperation. That's their survival instinct at work, too.

When children are babies, we smile at every wiggle and bubble and burp. When children get older, they can feed themselves, dress themselves, and go to the bathroom alone or with very little help. We tend to forget that they need encouragement and praise for these accomplishments. We must make an effort to remember. You appreciate being thanked or noticed for what you accomplish at work, even though it's "just your job," right?

Out on the street, we rarely hear parents complimenting their children, and when we do, it's usually something like "You look so pretty today," or "Oh, aren't you the cowboy!" It's usually about how they look or how well their behavior suits the parent's mood at the moment. Cute and quiet won't take a person very far, and when cute fades and quiet explodes, what's left to support a positive self-image?

Compliment young children on their drawings and songs and, sure, on their clothes if they picked them out. But complement them *too* for patient behavior, cooperation, and other things that are going to be hard to grow into. Patience and cooperation require ego-loss, and it's hard for children who are just finding out who they are and how they fit in to give that up.

This is why young children are so possessive about toys. Their things become part of their identity, and they need safe times and places to work through that, to discover that there's more to them than what they *have*. Some of us never got that reassurance and never made that discovery, which is all the more reason to make sure our children do.

Children live in the here and now. The Future is a nearly impossible concept for them to grasp. An hour is an enormously long time to a young child. A week is infinite. In fact, those sorts of measurements of time are not fully meaningful to children younger than 5 or 6, even if they can use words such as "hours" and "minutes" and "years."

When you praise your young child for qualities to come, you lay an important foundation. Perhaps your children can't yet understand what patience is, but they'll associate the word with behaviors that feel successful, and be inclined to repeat them. If you praise them for patient behavior, then when they can understand, they'll remember that you've always told them that they have it in them, and they'll be able to connect with it. Remember: "if that which you seek you do not find within, you shall surely never find it without."

While growing up, some people heard that they were lazy or stupid or greedy or perfect or some other oppressive rubbish. Children have so many ideas, too many coming too fast to notice them all, much less finish everything they start. This unbridled, undirected enthusiasm is common. Parents and teachers need to help children find suitable outlets and directions, help them find a path that energy can safely and creatively propel them along. Instead, that energy is all too often treated as conscious rebellion. Parents often expect or allow themselves to respond with considerable strictness and, usually, anger.

This is like coming across a natural spring and instead of seeing it as a potential well, calling it a leak in the river and trying to plug it up. None of our parents were the only ones to have stifled a child, and none of us is the only person to have bounced back from it. But it sure wasted a lot of time, didn't it?

Society would have us believe that parents and children will always be at odds. Well, actually, no, they won't. They don't have to be. We're meant to be *complements* to our children; we know this because the Gods' relationship is complementary, not hierarchical. Grown-ups and children aren't opposites, and needn't relate as opponents. After all, in the fullness of the cycles, we're the *same* people. And we're supposed to feel enriched, not threatened, by our children's growth.

We're meant to be regents, as Canyondancer and I see it. Whatever power we have over the Explorer's life is more like responsibility: to prepare him for independence, not to mold him into one of our visions. (It's not that we don't tout our visions, we just don't insist that he be equally captivated. That would be putting a condition on love, and that would be breaking faith.)

Parenting or teaching (or priesting, priestessing, or living) for "power-over" wastes time! If you feel compelled to be in charge of every aspect of young folks' lives, then maybe you need to look to the child within, who may still be needing something. The child without needs to find her or his own way, and teachers need to be coaches and fans, not designated hitters.

Patience, Please

Cast this spell, say or sing this rhyme, as often as you need to. Experiment with tunes and rhythms, tempos and styles, in accordance with the situations that provoke its use! (If the child's drumming-on-pots is incessant, try it "in reggae," for instance.)

> Patience with this energy
> Gracious Goddess, grant to me!
> Send your strength up from the Earth
> Help me balance impatience with mirth.

And when you feel like working with the energy a toddler can raise _so_ easily, try this:

> Energy, energy, rise and shine,
> Make a cone and go with mine!
> Send this joy and innocence,
> Round the Worlds, us all to bless.

Visualize a cherubic sort of halo around everything, make a cup of tea, and try to learn to _bask_ in this. It is, after all, all too fleeting.

Children between the ages of 1 and 5 will be ready to start learning some basic Craft techniques. Particularly useful to them will be the ways we've already seen to vent anger, ways to celebrate their own accomplishments, and some basic seasonal and elemental correspondences. As they begin to work more and more with words, we need to give them some of our vocabulary to work with!

In early childhood, children are working on understanding themselves as separate from their parents and siblings, and that their newly-grasped individuality is bound by limits. All of this is kind of kaleidoscopically perceived, too, because their conversion to linear time is not yet complete .

Some of their limits are physical: they may not run well yet, can't reach this or that. Others are social: they aren't allowed to touch this or go there. Any limitation is difficult to accept, and that frustration is generally expressed loudly, sometimes with broad gestures. When they can't act in the world the way they want to, they may throw tantrums because that's the only *action* left to them.

What children really need in the way of support, while they're going through this first round of identity establishment, is security. They have grown enormously from infancy in their first year, but they weren't conscious of those changes, which were mostly "pre-programmed." The difference between that growth and what they experience between the ages of 1 and 5 is like the difference between learning to drive (learning to work the levers and buttons and physically control the car) and learning to plan routes and book reservations for cross-country caravans.

In early childhood, children are learning the nature and extent of their power in the world, and while they are testing themselves, they need the world to be stable. While they perfect speech and motor control, they need dinner and bed to be at the same time every night. (If you're practicing jump shots from different positions around the court, you want the backboard to stay in the same place.)

Children need to be able to rely on their environment—including their caretakers. They need this stability for many years, and prefer it to last their whole lives. (Remember that children of most ages need special reassurance if there's a divorce: they need to be specifically told that it wasn't anything they did or didn't do that caused the split. They need this reassurance straightforwardly and often. Remember, too, that if you take your anger out on them, they can't believe you when you say it's not their fault.)

A parade of different baby-sitters is potential misery. In third grade, the Explorer's class had different substitute teachers almost daily for a whole semester, and it was an utterly wasted year, academically. (The Explorer learned a lot that year, but it wasn't what the school board planned for the grade-schoolers to learn.) Grown-ups sometimes encounter similar circumstances: one year the office I worked at employed four temporary secretaries, and until we hired someone permanently, routines remained shuffled and our productivity stayed low. We're all aware (aren't we?) that sleeping, eating, and going to the bathroom on a pretty regular schedule keeps us healthier our whole lives. Routines are very important.

When children have to reevaluate and reestablish basic relationships all the time, they don't have the energy or attention that growing up requires, and sometimes they get years past a stage of development without every really addressing the relevant issues. In this respect, Pagan teachers need to make an effort not to slow their students down.

Magical Security

Choose one or two basic routines: a table blessing, maybe, and a little song at bedtime; or an opening chant and story-time. Stick with them through sickness and health, changes of teachers, etc. Establish a regular God- or Goddess-time. Give students the security of routine in a sacred context as well as in everyday life, just as the Goddess or God gives us the security of the seasons and the months.

Little children like repetition. They like rhyming songs and poems: *ee-eye-ee-eye-oh* and *fee fi fiddly eye oh, oh, oh, oh.* These and other old favorites *are* favorites because they rhyme, repeat, and alliterate. Children like repeating rhythms, too. A 3 1/2-year-old

Four-year-old Ivy is allowed (with three-on-one adult supervision) to place
a tea light in a chalk circle she has drawn on the floor.

Witch-child in our community loved to sing just one line of a
chant: *Earth and Water, Fire and Air*, over and over and over.

By the age of 2 1/2, most children can learn simple verses,
and most like to sing. (It is also true that most of them can't stay
on key, or make subtle distinctions of tune. If they're awful by the
time they're 8 or 10, somebody will tell them—don't let it be
you.) Teach them our chants. *We all come from the Goddess, and to
Her we shall return* might be enough at first; they can learn the
rest later. They might even pick it up in Circle on their own.

Here's a little song that children can sing:

Full Moon Song

When I see the Moon all full and bright,
I know there's gonna be a Circle tonight.
Mom and Dad and me and the people I love
raise our Athames to the Moon up above.
White Moon, bright Moon, Mother of Life,
shine me a kiss down the blade of my knife.

You can start to teach basic Craft etiquette to young children, too. You can teach them by example, of course: you can cast "little Circles" (fire-drawn and Quarter-called Circles, without full rites and invocations) and then let them practice cutting a door with their fingers. You can practice more Circle etiquette with the help of plush animal or other toy friends.

It is inappropriate for small children to have sharp athames, and physical danger is not the only consideration. Young children are not able to make the cutting distinctions the athame represents in associations to the East, nor can they be masters of the Fire it represents to Traditions that correspond it to the South. Fortunately, there are alternatives. The Explorer received a rightly-shaped wooden letter opener as his first athame. If you are uncomfortable with any sort of "knife," young children can use a wand or their fingers with a bit of salt and water dabbed on their fingernails to make the point.

Circle Etiquette Song

Mommy casts the Circle, Daddy draws it, too,
And if we want to leave it there's something we must do

We have to cut a Doorway with a finger or a blade
That way we do not disturb the Circle that we've made!

Mommy lays the Altar, Daddy builds it, too
Before you touch things on it, there's something you must do

You have to ask permission, before you touch a thing
That's how we show respect, Summer, Autumn, Winter, Spring.

Provided you're using "non-toxic" oil, we think it's fine to anoint children in the Circle; some oils that adults can tolerate might be uncomfortable for children (such as rosemary, which burns a little). We also think it's alright to pass them the wine during Cakes and Ale, assuming there is something non-alcoholic for them to drink if your Cakes and Ale are substantial. Children don't usually like wine—it's an acquired taste—and can touch the cup to their lips or taste a drop on their fingertips if they don't want a whole sip.

If your child "spooks" and doesn't want to be anointed, or partake in Cakes or Ale, that's okay, as it is okay if *you* are uncomfortable with their participation. There are alternatives. Anoint the air above his head or the ground at his feet, and make a libation of his portion of the Cakes and Ale. We *all* have that option in any Circle, and it's important for our children to know that.

Cakes and Ale and Children

SADD (Students Against Drunk Driving) and MADD (Mothers Against Drunk Driving) argue vehemently that *ever* allowing underage people even a *sip* of alcohol is child abuse. Families in Europe start their children on table wine at an early age. Clearly, it's a cultural question.

If you're teaching other people's children, know how their parents feel about Cakes and Ale for them, so that your work supports what they're learning at home. Give the question *and* the children due consideration so that your decision's not arbitrary or dogmatic. There is no single right answer. You will need to decide—as a parent and as one of the Elders to whom the children in your Pagan community can turn for advice and example—how you feel about children sipping from the Circle's chalice.

Making robes for young children is, likewise, optional. Children are symbolically oriented, though they aren't analytical and can't talk about symbols the way we can. They can "understand" anointing, and they can "understand" the communion of Cakes and Ale.

The children you work with might "understand" wearing robes, or they might not. If they know that the adults in the community work robed, then having their own robes might be an encouragement. One couple in our coven has a daughter, who just turned 4. She wants her own Cord (she calls it a "Rope"), but she doesn't want to wear it, or even join the Circle, every time. That's fine— I feel the same way! Children often have their own ideas about what's appropriate to wear in Circle, and they're quite occasionally right!

They may want to wear dressy secular clothing, or they may want to adorn themselves in strange get-ups. Remember that the reason to wear non-ordinary clothes in Circle is that apparel is a powerful cue as to time and place and focus. Children step between the worlds with less effort than it takes most adults, and what cues us may not be as important to them. If your child feels reverent in something eccentric, so mote it be. Particularly at Sabbats, it's perfectly proper—magically and socially—to let the children's imaginations choose their "robes."

Selecting robes, or material for them, is a chance to reinforce color associations. Children often have their own associations, and if they are not "orthodox," it's still good to honor

Skye's faerie robe is just the right one!

them. Children naturally understand the *idea*, and if they make their own choices, their self-confidence is bolstered. Some children will be interested in helping to make robes, and others will not. That's okay—a lot of adult Witches buy robes or have them made. But don't overlook this opportunity to let children know that sewing robes (or capes, altar cloths, tunics, and festival costumes, etc.) is an honorable enterprise among brothers and sisters of the Craft.

Socially, sewing and other "domestic skills" are heavily gender stereotyped and this is a very practical arena in which to challenge those stereotypes. The knowledge of sewing carries the knowledge of other things, too. Knowing how to sew is knowing how to understand and follow instructions, it's an understanding of spatial relationships, it's a tool of creativity. By all means, encourage the children in your community to try!

Sewing is not only admired and respected among us, it's also a bartering skill. A generation well-supplied with such skills could alter the economy as well as its own clothes!

Making a Robe

An easy way to make a robe for a child is to buy a piece of material 36 inches wide and twice the height of the child, and fold it in half, right sides together, lengthwise. Lay it down on the floor and ask your child to lay down on top of it, shoulders an inch or two below the fold, arms out to the sides, legs spread (like DaVinci's *Vitruvian*).

With chalk, outline your child's arms, making the sleeves either straight or belled at the wrist depending on how yours look. Make the skirt full enough to let the child's legs stretch. Be sure to make marks at each side of the child's neck, too, so you'll know where to cut a head-hole.

Cut along an imaginary line about an inch away from your chalk marks, and sew the sides and arms (remembering not to sew the arm holes closed). Cut a slightly crescent hole between the neck-marks on the fold, and in the center of that curved opening, on what will be the front of the robe, cut a slit 3 or 4 inches long.

Finish the hem of the robe and the hems of the sleeves as you would any robe's hems. Around the neck, you can either

Mom and Priestess Sue outlines Rowan with chalk, drawing a robe pattern on the fabric.

just roll the fabric down and tack it in place, or you can use seam binding. Even if you're a beginner, this project shouldn't take very long once you've brought the fabric home.

Use your imagination in selecting the fabric. Black or white or any other color you normally use for robes is fine, but there are also printed fabrics available that might appeal to you. Children's energy is different from adults' and it's alright if their robes aren't identical. Particularly, if your children have a strong preference, feel free to invoke "strength through diversity" when you're making their robes.

If you are working with a large group of children, have a robe-making party! If the children you're working with are so inclined, let them decorate their robes with fabric paints, inscribing symbols of power that are meaningful to them around the hem or at the bottom of the sleeves. Children between the ages of 1 and 5 can't handle sewing machines, but they can choose thread colors and make poppet clothes from the scraps. They can dance to background music while you sew, putting the energy of joy into their robe. The more fun they have helping make their own robes, the more reverent they can be when they wear them.

Robed or in other outfits, children are naturally attracted to (small c) circles, too—after all, they spent the first nine months of their lives in an ovoid nursery. Children like to twirl, and be swung in circles; they like to be encircled in the arms of trusted adults, too. And circles are natural illustrations of much in Wicca.

You may have to draw or trace circles you want to use with young children, because they don't develop the motor precision to draw circles until they're between 4 and 6, and even then they can be wobbly. If you have space and time to draw a circle outside, in dirt, sand, or even gravel, you can set up the ol' stick-and-string, and youngsters *can* help draw the circle. Once drawn, this circle can be divided in many ways—in half, to talk about night and day, Winter and Summer. In quarters to talk about the Quarters, the seasons, the Elements. Such circles can be decorated, they can be filled with drawn or collected symbols, they can be stood in and Quarter-appropriate songs sung or dances danced.

The Wheel of the Year

An easy way to begin is with holidays: Yule, Ostara, Harvest, Samhain. These four will interest young children the most because they are the most obvious. (We rather like the double combination of agrarian and astronomical holidays here. A nice integration, and so natural.)

If you draw on posterboard or mark out on the ground, a circle on which you place symbols of the holidays with which children are most familiar (Go ahead, put their birthdays on it, too!), they're likely to ask what goes at the ends of the other spokes. And if the children don't ask, you can wonder aloud. (On cement, use chalk or masking tape; the tape will also work on most carpets and tile floors, too.)

When your students are ready and interested, you can add arrows to the Wheel to show which way it turns, so that they can use the Wheel as a sort of calendar: if we've just done the jack-o'-lantern, then we must be on our way to the Yule tree. (When they're older, you can use circles on the ground to show them how the Moon and planets move around the Sun.)

If you let your students choose symbols that make sense in their minds, the Wheel you show them will teach them more, whether it's a symbol to keep or one to erase when you're finished. If you're not saving whatever project you've worked on, consider taking a picture. I guarantee it'll make an interesting bit of history, and an appropriate entry or illustration for your child's first journal and an eventual Book of Shadows. Besides, children understand that if you're taking pictures of something, it's important. Most children like to catalogue their activities and accomplishments, too.

We all like our accomplishments to be recognized, no matter how old we are. For little children, it's especially important because they don't have enough experience or knowledge to tell themselves when they've got it right. The best advice that "child experts" can give us these days is not to *exaggerate* your praise—little children are inexperienced, not stupid—but to be lavish with *real* praise. "You did it!" or "Gee, that's tidy," or "You're taking good care of your doll," or "Fluffy seems to enjoy that," are the sorts of things to say.

We read something once that said you should never praise children by expressing personal approval of what they're doing. "I'm so happy when you remember to ask to go to the bathroom" might be absolutely true when you're working on toilet training, and we don't think there's anything wrong with saying so—as long as that's not the *only* kind of praise the child hears.

The point is to avoid creating a dependency that keeps children from feeling good about anything they do unless it meets with your or somebody else's approval. It's great when parents and teachers *do* approve of what children are doing, but children also need to make different choices than their parents and teachers could or would. They need to know that "success" and "achievement" and general "goodness" don't come from other people's judgments (or what they imagine other people's judgements will be).

Focus on the child's achievement in its own terms. "You've been concentrating on that for a long time," or "You certainly worked hard on that," or "That came out just the way you wanted it to," are encouraging things to say—whether your students are young or grown. Pointing out things like that sets up a healthy yardstick for the children to measure themselves by, as they grow and become more conscious of their identities and their places in the world.

When little children fall down, or can't do something they've been trying for a while, acknowledge their feelings. "Oh, I bet *that* makes you angry," or "Gosh, that probably hurts!" acknowledges the feelings and lets the child know that other people recognize those feelings. (Checking back with the Explorer, we find he remembers that it really annoyed him when we responded that way—he felt it made "too big a deal" of his spills. Failure is a valid part of our experience and it must be acknowledged: even Michael Jordan didn't score every time he shot.)

It is also important to recognize children's growth. Our culture doesn't have many ways of doing that, especially with young children. Their experiences range from being called "little" until they're teen-aged and then being expected to develop adult attitudes and habits virtually overnight, to being pushed into a grown-up role when a baby brother or sister is born.

Humans have the longest childhood of any mammal. There's a reason for this: we have a greater capacity and need to *learn* than other mammals, because we have a greater capacity for learning, and a lot more *to* learn. Expecting a young child to understand, interpret, and act as a miniature grown-up is both cruel and useless. The fact is that we humans are children emotionally and socially longer than we are children sexually. No matter how big or precocious preschoolers may be, they still need babying sometimes. (We all do.) Children will grow up at their own pace, and you'll be most helpful to them if you recognize that and "go with the grow." When there is a milestone in a student's life, a milestone of maturity, celebrate it, even if it's not a conventional passage. What matters to your students should matter to you.

One way to offer recognition is in a Circle, cast as formally or informally as feels right. Be sure it's big enough to embrace all the friends and family invited. (And don't take it personally if your kid is shy and doesn't want to. They don't have to take part; and you can have the ceremony even if they're ignoring you or watching from outside the Circle.)

Before you start, collect a few symbols of each Quarter—perhaps one or two mugs or cups for West, for instance, some paper fans or toy birds for East, etc. Keep these gifts inexpensive, but intriguing, and when you collect them, keep the children's understanding of correspondences in mind.

You can do such a ritual for one child or for several. Our "ideal scenario" is one in which a class of children are brought into a Circle, honored as a group by the whole community, and then honored again, individually, at home by their families. But there are other ideal scenarios—like yours! Young children's image-and-symbol orientation gives us opportunities like this to impress memories of a distinctively Pagan culture, and we ought to take them.

Now You're Getting Bigger

Bring the children into the Circle in your usual way, or in a way that seems appropriate to the occasion. Recite this rhyme:

> Now that you're (5) and growing up
> You get to meet the Quarters

And learn that they give gifts to all
The Lady's sons and daughters.

Introduce the children to Quarters, saying something like, "Greetings, Watchtowers of the Direction. Here are children to meet you and learn from you." Then let each child choose *one* gift from each direction. When this is done, share milk and cookies in a brief Cakes and Ale period, and then close the Circle with a big hug. Parents, keep these gifts for your child.

Children don't do magic the way grown-ups do, but children as young as 2 or 3 years old work with spell-forms pretty naturally. They're inclined to rhyme and repeat, and although their imagery isn't adult, it can be very intense. There's nothing at all wrong with encouraging this natural ability. You—and later, they—must realize that little children are learning forms and developing concentration, but are not capable, for some years, of working full-fledged magic.

When young children are beginning to explore their magical aptitude, they can't make ethical judgments for themselves. It's up to you to teach them what we think is the most important thing about magic: before they do any for anybody else, they have to ask and get permission. (There are exceptions, but start with the general rule.)

You can teach this in all kinds of mundane circumstances: if your child discovers a favorite toy is broken and brings it to you to fix, you can say something like, "Do you want me to mend Mr. Fluffy-bunny's ear, or shall I just hold him? Do *you* want a hug?" This is an example of asking before you do "magic" for anyone, and reminds us that needs can differ. Be on the lookout for opportunities to teach the idea that magic *isn't* always appropriate: "Oh, Mommy, can we do magic to make the dinner cook faster?"

We do NOT recommend (and indeed, caution against it) that you ask "Ms. or Mr. Dinner" if it's alright to do faster-cooking magic for them. There's a rash of sentient-food advertising on the airwaves right now giving the impression that food does not want to be eaten. Wiccans need to think about this—and whatever similar problems arise in the future—because *we* say that the

God dies so that we can live, willingly, and unafraid because He'll be reborn, so that we can live. We think it's best to bring these things up to our children so the subliminal social messages from Madison Avenue don't overwhelm our children's developing Wiccan perspectives and perceptions.

(Teddy Grahams commercials were the first examples I jotted down in my diary. A preschooler talks to the teddy-shaped bites of his cereal, pretending first to rescue them from drowning in his glass of milk, and then munching them with glee. But the M&Ms commercials, and Der Wienerschnitzel commercials, are more familiar examples.)

The purpose of a spell is to toss an intention onto the surface of life's pool and let it be realized as the ripples reach the shore. (This is more than metaphor: many a spell's been cast by tossing an energized pebble into a pond.) Children tend to *assume* a connection between their ideas and the world at large. This is why they have so much trouble with the distinctions we make between "reality" and "fantasy." It's also why it's so easy for children to blame themselves for things that happen around them. When children are young, we have a wonderful chance to direct them away from that guilt and into confidence. Use some of the spells in this book, and write your own; and when your students are older, help them create their own.

Spell to Heal a Friend

After you've made sure it's okay to work magic for this friend, say,

> Ground and flame, wind and rain
> Help (my friend) be well again.

(Include the friend's name if you can.)

Turning around slowly, your children can clap hands while they recite this the number of times that corresponds with the friend's age (If the friend is 6 years old, recite it six times). It never hurts to jump with both feet at the end of a spell, or add this couplet:

> With harm to none
> Let this be done.

Wicca's spells tend to be rhymed; it's a memory aid. Rhymes are easy to learn: energy that's not used trying to remember what to say next is energy that can power the magic. Children love rhymes, and are generally comfortable knowing that they can influence the world, as long as they are assured that not *everything* that happens is the result of their work. Children can put "good" out—like kitties and puppies, they can hardly help it—but they're not "strong" or disciplined enough to magically cause calamity. They need frequent reassurance on this point, too, because their feelings can seem *very* powerful to them.

A great deal of social and religious institutions put restrictions on behavior, and knowing the rules of behavior empowers us. We might not be able to control our behavior appropriately the first few times we go to a place that has unfamiliar rules, but we learn. The distinction between doing magic in the Circle and venting frustration outside the Circle is a useful one; as we get older, we understand "Circle" figuratively as well as literally. But literally is where we all start.

Knowing that magic is what happens in a Circle, and what they think or say outside is not magical, is reassuring to children. As adults, we know that we *can* do magic outside a Circle; but as adults, we also know that as children discover their human powers they tend to think they're somehow responsible for everything. They have very little experience of things being otherwise. Giving them a very clear sense that only what they do in Circle counts as magic helps them to know that shouting "I hope you get hurt" at Billy Pushes-people-into-walls did *not* make the car hit Billy.

Giving this assurance to children is a fine opportunity to let them know that when grown-ups do spells, we usually include a "disclaimer," because we do not want our will to do anyone else harm. The idea is that our perspective is limited, whereas the perspective of the God or Goddess is not, and She can see ways of accomplishing things that are unimaginable for us. We focus on the result we intend to achieve, imagining it done, and leave doing it to the God or Goddess. This may seem difficult to explain to small children, but it *is* possible.

How Spells Work

"We express our will quite clearly to the Goddess (or God) and leave it up to Her to find a way for it to happen without hurting anyone else," may be too abstract for young children to understand. Here's a way of putting it that will be easier to grasp: "When you want to go somewhere in the car, you tell Mom or Dad, and you let them decide what's the best way to drive there without going where the road is blocked or getting into accidents."

One problem some grown-ups have with spell-work is that many of us were taught when *we* were children that it was not polite to ask for things for ourselves. Lots of Witches who are quite comfortable working spells to heal friends, for world peace, or for someone else's success are reluctant to work for their own gain. It isn't wrong to not use magic for yourself, but it's perfectly alright to *do* so, too. Many Witches who are raising their children to the Craft today were raised to believe that attention to your own success is selfish.

Children are naturally selfish, which means that they naturally pay attention to their own needs and wants. This is no moral flaw, no matter what anyone's been taught. If children can't pay attention to themselves, they can't master themselves: they will never learn to feed themselves or walk or go potty like a big girl or boy. If children don't pay attention to themselves, they will never come into their power.

Some adults, it must be admitted, don't want children to be empowered, but generally speaking, Witches do. Wicca teaches that we are all God or Goddess, which, in this context, means that we're all (potentially, at least) capable of taking care of ourselves and of developing and maintaining healthy relationships with life, the Universe, and everything. If you trust that, you won't want such a tight rein kept on the children, because their creative freedom and growth won't seem threatening to you. Some of us can remember our own parents' jealousy when we went beyond their accomplishments, or their insistence that we take the path they didn't dare to follow. If your children's awareness of their needs and diligence in efforts to meet those needs threaten you, then you need to nurture your own inner child, not discourage your son's or daughter's efforts. If your children surpass you, congratulate them and have a little bask in their glory, because you earned it.

Between the ages of 1 and 5, children face doing a lot of new things. Sometimes this unnerves them. We all get excited when we face new situations. Witches usually ground and center, do a little ritual, wear a little magic in a pouch—but we had to be taught to do that, and the younger generations need to be taught to do it, too.

Even when a child has done something or been somewhere or talked to someone once or twice, it may be overwhelming until they have more experience "under the belt." This can take a while. If your youngster is shy or nervous, give him or her time to come into their own. If you want children to outgrow their childhood awkwardness, don't label them with it!

Spell to Feel Good About Yourself

I am God (or Goddess), this is true
There's something good in all I do.
If I make mistakes today
God (or Goddess) loves me anyway!

The neatest way to cast this spell on yourself is to gather a handful of packing peanuts, confetti, flower petals, sequins (anything you like, as long as you're willing to clean it up) and fling it into the air while you say the last line. Water sprinkled over yourself from a bowl works nicely, too, especially on hot days.

Spell for Doing New Things

Here I go, try something new
I'm not sure what I should do
So I will watch and learn and grow
Time will tell and practice show.
Earth and Water, Fire and Air,
Help me will and help me dare.

Although older children may be able to do spell-work on their own, we think it's a good idea for children's religious observances and magics to be supervised for several years. Until you are sure your children have a clear understanding about the ethics and "physics" of working magic, it's not fair to expect them to protect themselves. Even when they're old enough to practice on their own, we think it's a good idea for parents (or another responsible Pagan adult) to discuss the children's work with them before and after they do it. This is something adults often do with their own priests or priestesses, so it establishes that good habit in our children. It also gives them our support in their quest for independence.

Later Childhood

Age

6 to 11 years old

Developmental Needs/Work/Challenges

Identity and independence, trust of adults other than parents, exploration of world outside home, reason and skepticism, trial and error, reassurance of worth

Aspects of Wicca

Secrecy and privacy, directional/tool associations and uses, color associations/uses, chants, seasonal and Traditional stories, some history, some comparative religion, simple herb work

Society encourages us to take power over children. Legally, parents are held responsible for what children do, and where there is responsibility, there must be power. (This is also true of the responsibility we want children to accept: they have to have power—authority—before they can be responsible for its exercise.) The dominant paradigm insists that power rightfully belong to a select few; Witches tend to think that we're all naturally powerful.

If we take power *over* children, we (unrealistically) expect to control every aspect of their lives indefinitely (or else we expect to let go on their 18th birthday, cold turkey, and that's hard for everybody involved). The problem is that if *anybody* else has control over every aspect of somebody else's life, that person has no life—and the relationship, to say the least, suffers.

If we take power *with* children we can see that, although grown-ups do most of the directing, children contribute a tremendous amount of energy to work with. If we are patient and sensitive to the lessons our children are learning through us (and directly from the Mother), young students can learn to be genuinely effective in a remarkably short period of time.

Children learn how to use language before they understand what particular words mean. They work with patterns of speech, picking up on structure first and analysis later. They also pick up on concepts such as privacy and secrecy before they understand the range of circumstances the concepts involve.

The notion that secrecy and privacy have sound foundations in the philosophy of magic is irrelevant to most children, and is generally beyond the capacity of those younger than 7 or 8 years of age. (The way you have to think about things, in order to see the connections, is not paved in younger children's brains yet, just as the height they need to reach the top shelf hasn't grown yet.) For children, as well as for many Witches, secrecy and privacy are hot issues. Any number of court cases have challenged Wiccan parents, wondering whether it can be good for children to come up in a faith that has to be kept secret. In this respect, secrecy does about as much harm as comes to birthday celebrants who keep their wishes secret. It's ignorance that's the problem, not secrecy; most religions restrict access to some relics or knowledge. It's not much different than having to pass basic math courses before you can enroll in calculus or physics.

It is the nature of life that there are mysteries. One way to describe the polarity on which Wicca is based is as "the Known and the Mysterious." We are each partly known and partly hidden—to and from ourselves as well as to and from others. It is crucial that Wiccan parents and teachers respect the mysteries within our children. (For more about actually explaining secrecy to children and other people, please see *The Family Wicca Book* [Llewellyn, 1993].)

We think the best way to approach this subject and related issues is with reference to children's own experience. Most children have felt magically special at one time or another; they were bedazzled by something (a thought, the song of a bird, a character in a book, a snatch of music, a surprise, etc.).

Most children can understand that this feeling can't be shared. It can be referred to, but only faintly described, because words just don't work. That means that the experience is secret, because you can't tell anyone else *all* about it. This is what you can call a Wonderful Secret. There are lots of things we can't understand without knowing some other, more basic things first. Calculus, for example, is unintelligible, hidden from us (secret and occult) without basic math. There are some things that are "secrets" because we do not yet know enough to understand them, and those things are also what you can call Wonderful Secrets. Still another sort of Wonderful Secret is the surprise! Your friends leap out from behind the couch and yell, "Happy birthday!" when you turn on the light. Those are hard secrets to keep, but a lot of fun in the end.

Private thoughts, feelings, and fantasies aren't always entirely wonderful, but they are always okay. Their energy is ours, and as long as we use our energy responsibly, we don't need to feel guilty about any of our feelings. As Wiccan parents and teachers of Wicca, we must make ourselves easily available to our children when they need to talk about their feelings, happy or scary.

There are, of course, Awful Secrets. We believe that Awful Secrets—secrets that give you the "uh oh" feeling, secrets that make your stomach hurt—should be told, and told until they're *dealt* with. In some elementary school programs, children are taught not to keep *any* secrets. This is an effort in the prevention of sexual abuse, and should be respected. At the same time, children need to learn that the either/or understanding of the world (the source of blanket statements beginning with "never," "always," "none," "all," etc.) is not the *only* way to see the world.

It's risky to put things in such absolute terms, too. It makes it much too easy for older children to blow off everything you say when they find a flaw in one pronouncement. As children go through their "law and order" stage, they examine everything you say—not with the intention of discrediting you, but to get a handle on the world. As Witches, we know perfectly well that the world isn't "absolute" in the either/or, black/white, good/bad sense, and it makes sense to avoid, as much as possible, giving our children the impression that it is. (It's a tricky balance, because there are some things that for a while at least, are absolutely forbidden to little children, and others that are absolutely required of them. But then again, all magic is "a tricky balance.")

It's wonderful when children make these connections, when they start recognizing and anticipating patterns, and noticing when a different element is introduced. Before explaining the exceptions you're making, praise your children for noticing the rule. This will reinforce their growing perception of things as connected, and secrecy having a legitimate place in the order of things, and privacy being a fundamental right and realistic expectation.

Secrecy/Privacy Affirmation

Use this affirmation whenever there are secrets to be kept and privacy to be asserted. Modify it to meet your children's needs. In this, we affirm not only the individual's right to privacy and to keep his own counsel, we also affirm the individual's responsibility to respect other people's similar rights.

> Some things I share.
> Some things I do not share.
> Some things I decide about sharing.
> I can keep those things in my memory.
> I can keep those things in my room.
> I am safe. My privacy is safe.
> Perfect love and perfect trust.

When introducing this affirmation to students, take time to discuss it thoroughly. Children at this age need lots of real-life examples to set parameters of meaning. Talk about what you mean by "things." Talk about ways of sharing, and how you can decide whether you want to share something or not. Talk about exceptions to privacy. Use examples from your experience and their own. The group will come up with its own questions and discussion topics. Don't overlook anybody's concerns.

Keeping Secrets

- ❧ Are secrets always bad?
- ❧ Is keeping a secret always bad?
- ❧ How can you tell what sorts of secrets are okay to keep?
- ❧ Do you have any secrets?
- ❧ How do you feel about keeping your secrets to yourself?
- ❧ Do you know other people who have secrets? What do you think about that?
- ❧ How do you know when to keep somebody else's secret and when to tell a grown-up you trust?

Are children's realities always so "heavy"? No. Happily, they're not. One of the most real parts of children's lives, at this stage, is the part with pets in it. There are lots of things a child can learn from a pet, and from being a caretaker of an animal. The discipline and skills required will come in handy for at least one lifetime. What a child can learn about priorities and relationships is useful, too, although connecting "having a dog" to other relationships later on will need your guidance.

A great thing about dogs and cats is that they reach their adult size fairly quickly, and if children are 5 or 6 when they get a small animal, they'll probably be able, once the animal gets big, to remember how small it used to be. Apart from demonstrating that babies are *unlike* their parents in youth, and will be *like* their parents when they grow up, the "puppy experience," no matter what young animal you have, also lays the groundwork for an understanding of linear time. Children may have "yesterday," "today," and "tomorrow" down reasonably well, but a sense of continuity is slower to develop.

First ideas about events in time are kind of like a trail of spotlights on a dark stage, and between the ages of 6 and 10, children are lighting up the whole area, or beginning to, anyway. Children can remember things earlier than they can connect the memories; first memories are almost always stark vignettes, with no associations or connections with other memories. It takes a while for children to have significant insight about current events based on the memories of past events. Pets are reference points and can help us change the way we think about time. This is perfectly appropriate, because time, being an aspect of the mortal realm, is in the dominion of our Lord of the Animals.

Since animals have been domesticated, children have been learning about birth, love, and death from them. The bond between humans and other animals is very strong: there's not only our own Horned Sorcerer, but Disney's animated casts, myths and legends from every culture, and perennially popular stories about animals crossing wide times and distances in service to their human companions.

Which is not to say that humans haven't done their service to our animal Elders: midwestern North American tribes dance the buffalo back to life, their part in an ancient contract with the herds. Globally, most tribes hunt ritually, and in many cultures it's been common to claim various animal clans as kin. In His animal forms, the God's death in the service of life is ritually honored around the Wheel.

One of our honorary coveners, Grianwydd (say it "Grenneth"), promotes the "adopt-a-greyhound" program, and warns us *not* to get puppies or kittens at pet shops, which are supplied by now-infamous "puppy mills." Having seen too many pets be the victims of overly romantic owners, and much as we love comic strips like *Mutts* and *Peanuts,* we strongly caution, too, against anthropomorphic fantasies. Dogs and cats are not four-footed, furry little *people* who think and perceive as we do. They are sensitive to our moods, respond supportively to us, and they absolutely form attachments; they have feelings.

But they don't plan and they do not contemplate philosophy. Their psychology is behavioral, not Freudian. We love our beasts *and* we recognize that they are aliens, another species, seeing the world differently, moving through it with a different agenda, without even knowing it. Far from making our relationship with Milo and Hal and Bette Noire (the cats) and Barleycorn (the dog) at all clinical or distant, understanding this really cranks up the awe in which we hold them. We enjoy emphasizing the inter-species friendship theme, too; we think it's a good Wiccan attitude toward differences.

Furry or finny, feathery or leathery, new pets *can* be pains in the anatomy; but they *will* be teachers and blessings if you let them be, so here's a blessing for your pets.

New Pet Blessing

A group of children and their pets can participate in this ritual. Set aside a space and time for this ritual, ideally in a place that the children can spend time with the animals. A park is a nice place, as is the backyard of someone's home (if children have a chance to play there with their pets). If your children are old enough to learn this verse, they can each recite it alone, or they can say it in unison (more or less) with a group. Otherwise, they can repeat each line after adults say it. Use any Goddess and God names you like, of course:

> Earth and Water, Fire and Air
> Bless the pet that I bring here.
> I'll take care as best I can
> With my heart, and head, and hand.
> Herne and Diana bless us so
> Both together we can grow.

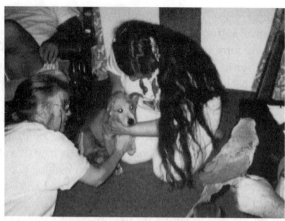

O'Gaea and a covener help Barley (the dog) and G.B. (the macaw) get ready for a pet blessing. Animals like these need lots of help and constant supervision to get along.

So many Witches have pets that local "classes" for children, about pet care, could be appropriate. From an afternoon's workshop to obedience classes or play groups, the range of possibilities is wide. A local Pagan pet show would be fun. Check with your local parks department—it might not cost a thing to reserve a corner of the park one afternoon and schedule a pet show. Collect some non-perishables for the food bank, or donations to a pet shelter, and take the opportunity to give prizes in Pagan categories such as the "blackest cat" or the "most mythical name."

Animal Associations

Animals have long been part of many intra-natural associations. Different aspects of the Goddess or God are associated with different animals: horses with Rhiannon, owls with Athena, stags with Herne, dogs with Hecate, fish with Llyr, serpents with Cernunos, and so forth. Animals also have Directional associations, and can represent qualities of the mind, qualities of the body, qualities of the spirit, and, of course, qualities of the psyche. There are also rich sociocultural associations: greyhound racing is the "sport of queens," for instance, and horse racing is the "sport of kings." It can be a lot of fun to explore those associations, current and mythical, with your children. You'll find a wide range of opportunities to discuss the less wholesome associations we make with animals, too. Talk to your children and your students about everything from the abuse of dog breeds like pit bulls terriers and rottweilers to the cruelty of rodeos and the irresponsibility of failing to spay and neuter.

Plants, too, are wonderful demonstrations of the ways of life. If you're working indoors with small children, a windowsill garden can be a marvelous classroom. If you can plant an outdoor garden, that's wonderful, but don't disparage the old milk-carton-in-the-window approach. Plants can teach a lot about growth and adaptation—not to mention time and life-cycles.

One of our coveners, Rocky, recalls that when he was a child, once "in the Spring in Denver," that he "could feel the Sunflowers buzzing in my hand when I held their stalks."

At the top of the trail, a group of parents and children stop to talk about the plants, animals, and signs of the season they've seen on their hike.

The Explorer used to have little conversations with the trees in our front yard. Those experiences don't have to stop in childhood, or be dismissed as we get older, even though the mainstream says they probably do. Encourage students to cultivate and talk about their relationships with plants, wild and domestic. Where can you and your students meet plants? Your yard (or a friend's) might be a good place to start, but if it's not, visit parks, zoos, botanical gardens, nurseries, arboretums and environmental exhibits, and even shopping malls. If you harvest seeds from last year's dying flowers, you can talk about the way there's a seed of life in every death. You can have a conversation with older children about what the seeds of life might be. Children of any age can plant the seed and watch it grow. A young gardeners' journal can be the first of many magical journals the children in your community keep.

As long as you use *natural* metaphors, you can turn them into learn-by-doing exercises. Planting is a particularly appropriate theme, of course, and something that children usually like. Agriculture on any scale connects one gardener with every gardener—in different climes and times there are different growing concerns, but every gardener works to nurture growth. Gardening is also a fine introduction to North.

You can grow what you need for spells and potions, you can grow some (or all, if you're very lucky to live on enough arable land) of what you need for dinner. Children can grow (up) in a garden, too.

Garden Blessing

The Lady of Life and the Lord of Seeds
Shall give my garden what it needs.
In gentle Earth and breath of Wind,
I will plant it to begin;
They will bring the Rain and Sun
And I will harvest when it's done.

There are plenty of ways you can learn from working with plants. They are tremendously and creatively various in their survival and growth strategies. Learning what to expect in a garden, how the weather and the soil (Air and Earth), the Sun's light and the rain (Fire and Water) interact with the seed (Spirit) prepares you for life.

Learning to integrate all the information available and come up with sensible direction in your life is something a garden can help to teach, as well. Learning to pay attention to the environment and not plant what won't grow is a critical skill in every dimension. Canyondancer and I came to Arizona from Oregon; we both grew up with rose gardens on every corner! Growing roses in Arizona is certainly possible, but where we live, it takes a lot of water and artificial shade. Roses are not really comfortable here, and though some carefully tended ones survive, few grow wild because they don't really belong here.

We miss roses, but we're happier with native plants here, partly because they're less work, but mainly because it's nicer to be surrounded by the plants that like to grow here. Understanding the environment you're in, and knowing what your own limitations are in that environment, are useful your whole life. It's even more useful if you've known from early childhood that recognizing limitations (so you can focus on the possibilities) is a sign of strength, not weakness.

You can dry plants, you can press them and make a Book of Botanical Shadows. You can teach older children how to make simple teas. And even if you don't if you live near a big-water shore, don't forget seaweed! One or two Winter Solstices we cut decorations from sheets of dried seaweed so we could decorate the trees where we picnicked and leave the pretties there without harm to the animals that lived there and were likely to eat them.

Plants come in many colors. Even if you can't plant a rainbow where you live, you can explore the world of plants through library books, botanical gardens and arboretums, and even some of the shows you'll find on PBS. And because plant lore is so ancient and primary, the associations plants have to magical acts and qualities are many.

Plant Associations

Commonly, plants are associated with nourishment, healing and magic. Nourishment and healing deal with the physical body; magic takes care of everything else. There are plants (like roses, thyme, and bay) to fill dream pillows, to sweeten dreams or reveal the future. There are plants associated with happiness, such as catnip, morning glory, and lavender. For protection, people think of garlic and thistles. Plant associations can be as complex or as simple, as flamboyant or discreet, as you like. The important thing to keep in mind is that they are magical by virtue of their life and their direct connection with the Mother Earth.

Plants are a wonderful starting place for students of the Craft, especially for the young. Like animals, they grow quickly, so the points you're making don't get lost before they're made. As well as being taught practically, the Craft's correspondences—starting with animals and plants—need to be taught in various ways, because they symbolize interconnection. As students master the basics, they can take a multimedia approach.

Teaching Correspondences Through Word Games

Word games are good in cars and buses, at picnics, on rainy days, or during Cakes and Ale. They might also be used as "weapons" in a "combat challenge" on Sabbat feast, too. Prizes? Dictionaries or thesauruses! (A local British Traditional priest has created a Wiccan trivia game that's a lot of fun, too.)

- ❧ "The Hangman from the North." A variation on an old favorite, if the Hangman is from the North, then players know the word will be associated with that direction....

- ❧ "I'm heading to the East and I'm taking..." Grianwydd and I played this game as "I'm going to the Moon, and I'm taking...," and had to take things in alphabetical order, cumulatively. In this variation you take 13 things associated with the East or one of the other directions, and you don't have to follow the alphabet. You still have to recite what the other players are taking before you add your item to the growing list.

❧ "My path to the South is a *warm* path that *excites* me *passionately*," Player One might say. "My path to the South is a *sunny* path that *runs* across the *desert*," Player Two might offer. "My path to the South is a *dusty* path that *burns* my feet *strongly*," Number Three could say, using first an adjective, then a verb and then an adverb, noun, or other adjective to describe a path to the game's designated direction.

❧ Prepare or assign crossword puzzles that focus on a set of correspondences.

❧ The direction is West. One association is *water*, and the first player says that word. The next player must think of a "West word" that starts with *r*, the last letter of the previous player's word. (If that proves to be a stumper for too long, use the next-to-last letter. The point is to become familiar with the associations, not to stress out or feel stupid.) The second player might say *rushes*, a third might say *sadness*; and a fourth might say *seahorse*.

Something else children in later childhood are ready to understand is that there are other religions in the world, and that some of them are very different from ours. When introducing our children to comparative religion, we don't want to "bash" other faiths, and there's no need or reason to do so. We think the best way to approach this subject is to begin by looking at what all religions have in common.

Questions Religions Address

- ๖ Who am I?
- ๖ Where did I come from?
- ๖ How do I fit in?
- ๖ What is the fundamental nature of the universe?
- ๖ What is the purpose of life?
- ๖ Is there life after death?

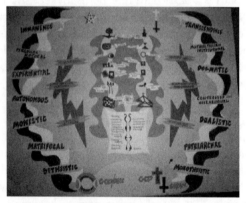

This display, made from posterboard, construction paper, glue, and markers, compares the points of Wicca and Christianity.

Different religions understand and answer these questions in different ways. To understand those differences, it is helpful to know that the world's religions developed at different times and in different places. One way students can learn is by creating a time line. On a chalkboard, on butcher paper, in a mural on the wall, on stickers attached to a map of the world, or even on ribbons you can roll up and tuck into a pouch, you can get a good idea of the continuity of history with a time line. Even if the times or distances are incomprehensible at first, the idea fascinates children between the ages of 6 and 11 years old.

The one included here is *very* basic. Over the next several years, students will be able to add to it, perhaps keeping a notebook with at least one page for every era, so they can make notes. This way, the picture in their mind of other ages and of the flow of history will get more detailed as they grow up.

The notes they take, the references they cite, will raise interesting questions to discuss now and when they're older, and any opinions or conclusions they record will be interesting to them later, too. It is, of course, possible to be very much more specific about most ages, and it's guaranteed that over the next several years we'll know a good deal more than we do now about very ancient times. Presentation of this, or any other time line, offers opportunity to talk about time being cyclical rather than linear, something else budding Witches need to know.

Time	Developments
EOLITHIC (Upper Paleo-) 35,000-12,000 B.C.E.	The Sorcerer at Les Trois Freres, Venuses at Willendorf. Flower Burials: concept of grave as womb. Craft said to start here.
PALEOLITHIC 12,000-7,000 B.C.E	Representations of Horned God.
NEOLITHIC 7,000-3,000 B.C.E.	Worship of Moon Goddess. "Little people" flourishing. Horned God taking on solar aspect. Writing develops for temple inscriptions. Hinduism develops.
THE IRON AGE 3,000-1,000 B.C.E.	Worship of Moon Goddess and Horned God. Britain's stone monuments built. Historical period for Old Testamnent.

IRON AGE (DYNASTIC TIMES) 1,000 BCE - 100 C.E.	Alexander the Great, Ptolemy I merge Greek and Egyptian pantheons; Isis predominates. Buddhism, Christianity develop.
THE FIRST FOUR CENTURIES C.E.	Consolidation of Pagan Traditions. Gradual imposition of Christianity; Mary promoted to Mother of God status. Charlemagne converts Pagan Saxons; Pagan practices begin to be banned.
THE MIDDLE AGES 5TH-12TH CENTURIES	European Pagan religions virtually wiped out.
THE BURNING TIMES 13TH-18TH CENTURIES	The Inquisition is established. Satanism develops in opposition to Christianity. New World colonized by Europeans.
MODERN TIMES 19TH CENTURY - THE PRESENT	Charles Godfrey Leland publishes *Aradia*; Margaret Murray's work is published; Gerald Gardner develops Wicca in 1950 –mid-20th century. The Gaia Theory develops late 60s, early 70s.

If time is difficult, space is not easy. By this we mean that it's hard to think about the whole world when we think about a particular time in history. When we think of the 15th century, for instance, most Wiccans think of the Burning Times—do we remember Leonardo Da Vinci or Columbus? Do we remember that the Anasazi ruins in northern Arizona are "medieval"? When we watch *All Creatures Great and Small* or read James Herriot's books, it's hard to remember that at the same time, the British were crowning Elizabeth II. With a time line stretched out you can study an era closely without forgetting its place.

Wiccan history is a wider field of exploration than you might imagine. Our lore and history are controversial anew with the 1999 publication of Ronald Hutton's *The Triumph of the Moon* (see "BurningTimes" in the Glossary). But history is certainly not Wicca's only—and probably not even its most—controversial facet. Hutton's scholarship is, for many American Wiccans, still obscure, but here's a controversy everyone's heard of: working skyclad.

Lots of festivals offer clothing-optional times and places, so even people who work robed or in street clothes are exposed (no pun intended, but go ahead and grin) to skyclad celebration. Many Traditions only robe if they've invited guests or are presenting ritual publicly. The joke explanation is that we all look great in candlelight (pretty much true). The serious explanations range from the Tradition's secret lore to the fact that the Goddess says that as a sign that we're truly free, we shall be naked in our rites.

We do our students a disservice if we don't go into this with them and help them deal with the popular perception that nudity is always sexual. If you've ever worked skyclad, you know this is utter nonsense, but the assertion is unsatisfying to people who haven't had the experience. It's not just to be fair to Wicca that we should talk about nudity, though. Unselfconscious respect for the human body and the amazing things it can do in the world is good for our children, too.

For the most part, our popular culture associates nudity with two things: inferiority and sex. If you're not naked for sex, then you're naked because you've been shamed; if "clothes make the man," then naked, you're "unmanned." These days, child porn is so much on people's minds that grandparents have to be careful about those naked-baby-on-the-rug pictures: take them to the drug store for developing and a panicky (or worse) clerk could call the cops!

Working skyclad, whether you do it or not, is still typical for a great many Wiccans, and sooner or later, any student of Wicca will

encounter at least the idea, if not the practice. Lingering perceptions of the body as a wicked instrument of sinful carnality, coupled
with the virulence of sexually transmitted diseases, make it a touchy
subject. These are associations that can make working skyclad difficult for people who are still coming to terms with their social
identities, never mind their sexual identities. So, anticipate that
your students will work skyclad at sometime in their lives, on their
own or with others, and lay the groundwork for other, *healthier*
associations. We think Wiccan associations with "beauty and
strength, power and compassion, honor and humility, and mirth
and reverence" are good for starters.

One psychological bugaboo about children seeing parents
naked is that children will notice that certain parts of adults'
bodies are *bigger* than those same parts on their little bodies,
and that this observation will stunt their self-esteem. We think
that unlikely, unless we call that difference shameful. (If somebody called your differences shameful, please go and talk it
through with a counselor. A good one will teach you how to
reprogram those "tapes" in your head. Your Priest or Priestess, if
you have one, will be happy to support your therapy, spiritually
and magically, when that's appropriate. But if they're not a professional counselor, don't expect professional counseling from
your Priestess or Priest.)

You may feel that Circling skyclad with children is not appropriate—certainly it's not okay everywhere and always. But it
is appropriate—and we think essential—to let children know
that everybody's body is beautiful and deserves respect. Nobody's
Craft name should be Inferio or Bulemia.

Skyclad Children

Whether or not you practice skyclad (or want to), it's an
up-front issue in the Craft, and if you are teaching, the question
will almost surely surface. Your students, for instance, will see
pictures of skyclad ritual in books by our most respected and
influential writers.

Here are some simple ways to lay a foundation for a child's growing understanding of nudity and sexuality as sacred:

- ❧ Attend a birth with your children. Hospitals and cable stations show videos.
- ❧ Grow plants from seeds.
- ❧ Visit an art museum (or your library's reference section for giant art books) and take a look at the classics.
- ❧ Introduce your children to candle baths.
- ❧ Discuss the importance of *not* teasing or criticizing children (or anyone!) about their bodies.
- ❧ Use real names for body parts and functions.
- ❧ Distinguish between moral judgment and physical consequence: don't tell children they'll go blind or grow hair on their hands; do tell them about AIDS and other sexually transmitted diseases.

If there's a chance for children in your community to witness birth, take it! The Explorer has been privileged to see not only photographs of his own home-birth, but to be present at two others. He has not seen other animals be born, except on PBS, but he has seen many newborn animals. (Please spay and neuter your animals. If you really want to show your kid small animals being born, call the Humane Society and see if they can help, or the zoo, or a local breeder. Don't breed pets to show children kitties or puppies being born.)

Most newborn animals, humans included, look very different from the adults of their species, and it's not just a matter of reduced size, either. Their proportions are different. The eyes of baby mammals are *huge* in comparison to the size of their heads, and all mammals respond parentally to all big-eyed babies. Most baby furry and feathery things have specialized baby-fuzz that may both protect them from heat or cold and act to camouflage them as part of the landscape. It isn't *meant* for babies to look like mom and dad right away.

You can even get some indirect help from the garden, instilling in your children the pride and confidence they'll need to work skyclad or do anything else they want to. In the garden you can appreciate the smallest leaves as well as the largest, you can see the way each plant reaches toward the Sun a little bit differently, a leaf tilted this way here, that way there. You can watch the poking-through leaves (cotyledons) actually "disrobe," dropping the husk to greet the sun with joyful naked leaves, a lot like many Wiccans disrobe to greet the Moon with joyful naked bodies.

You can wonder how the little plants feel with big ones all around, and listen to your children's answer to get an idea how *they* might be feeling, surrounded with big ones all around. Their concerns may not be psychological; they may just worry about getting stepped on!

It would be great if we didn't have to think ahead like this, it seems so "calculating." But we all have to compensate for the distortion in the idea that our bodies are in the way of our salvation. Children are naturally "cool with" their bodies until the culture shows them its current standards of beauty and worth. Since very few people meet the current standard without surgical help, it's easy to start thinking that our bodies are unworthy, and be embarrassed for other people to see them. Teenagers still have trouble with that in gym classes, in schools that still have gyms and P.E. It's important to facilitate our children's feeling good about their bodies.

Acorns Don't Provide Shade

Nobody *expects* an acorn to provide shade. Everybody knows you have to wait until the acorn's grown up into an "adult" oak tree before it does what trees do: make shade, make oxygen, keep the soil from eroding, provide shelter and food for other creatures. You could hold an acorn over your head, but you'd have trouble shading yourself with its little shadow, and in the meantime you'd be keeping it from germinating.

Children are not adults, either, but sometimes we expect them—and they expect themselves—to look and act like adults much sooner than they're capable. Children are *supposed* to be smaller than grown-ups. Our bodies grow slowly to give our brains time to learn the basics by the time our bodies are big.

Wicca teaches us that nothing is static. If you show your children how other things change as they grow, they will expect to change as they grow, too. If you remind them how much they have already grown—how much more they know and can do now than when they were born—then they will be secure in their expectation of growth. And then the differences between children's bodies and the bodies of grown-ups will be something to look forward to, not something to worry about.

What we want to convey to our children is that human bodies are not shameful, and need not be hidden because they are "nasty," but that our bodies are sacred and therefore beautiful and *private*, and ours to control. (Skyclad sure does make it clear that bodies come in many shapes, and a wider range of beauty, than the ones pop culture shows us.) There are many ways of looking at this question.

Working skyclad can be "for adults," just as driving and voting are "for adults." Working skyclad can be for the whole group because we all love and trust each other, because we are commanded to be naked in our rites. We're not *supposed* to all be the same, and we aren't. Some of us think it's okay to work skyclad with (or without) children, some of us don't. Some of us think working skyclad with our *own* children is a horrifying idea (and so do some of our children). Some find it challenging but not out of the question. Some think it's only appropriate if you start when the children are babies, some think it shouldn't be considered before they reach the age of majority.

When he was 10 or 11 years old, the Explorer started noticing the "sex and sensuality" jokes and comments that Pagans tend to make when gathered. For a few months, it offended him. The impression he had (that Pagans are no different than anybody else in thinking sex is all there is to bodies) had to be balanced! Because he had no access to skyclad Circles, he had no experience of his own to balance the bad impression he was getting. We had to talk about it openly and directly.

One factor that influences people's opinions on the subject is how they were brought up to feel about the human body; another factor is the Tradition of Wicca they practice: for some Witches like to dress up for ritual instead of undressing. But another significant factor is the atmosphere where you live. There are places where the anti-Witch sentiment is quite strong, and neighbors really can't be trusted not to spy or not to call the local Child Protective Services if the child mentions seeing grown-ups naked. If you're in such a situation, don't take chances.

She asks naught of sacrifice, She assures us in Her charge. Having your children taken from your home, having charges of child molestation or endangerment on your record, doing time for such charges, etc., is exactly the kind of sacrifice She asks naught of. If you practice skyclad, and can't let your children in on those Circles, cast other ones that they can see. If even that's too dangerous, stick to nature walks and PBS and cable channel information—that's a fine foundation, too, and eventually the circumstances will change.

Whatever you're wearing, and whoever you're telling, it's important that what *you* think and do is consistent with your interpretation of Wicca. Our cosmology is one of inter-connectedness; we believe that everything fits together synchronistically. To us, that means that our thoughts and feelings should fit together, too. It is not that what we feel and how we see the world should be in accordance with someone else's vision, necessarily, it's that our thoughts and presumptions need to be coherently whole in themselves.

When we have to isolate some of our opinions or habits from all the others because they don't fit, it's a sign that there's work to be done. Sometimes even when it's easy to imagine other people learning from their mistakes, it's still hard to imagine that we won't get in trouble for ours. Then we need to bring our feelings about our own mistakes into line with the idea that they're chances to learn, not tickets to hell. (We need to remember that as Wiccans, we don't believe in hell!) The way we put things when we think about them is something we learn when we're young, and those phrasings are hard to unlearn later on.

That's why it's so important not to plunge our children into the confusion we had to wade through—and may still be wading through!

Dancing the Maypole is a healthy way of sharing bodies. These youngsters are ready to dance their Maypole for the first time.

Witches tend to think that the *process* of growth is just as important, if not more important, than specific stages or rates of growth. So we don't feel like failures if we have to work at something, we feel like we're doing important work. Most of us are doing this "inner work," and it's perfectly alright to be doing that while you're teaching the stuff you *do* have a handle on.

There are, of course, things to be private about other than one's body, although it's of *paramount importance* that children know they do not have to share their bodies in ways that make them uncomfortable. For children of any age, trust is a fundamental issue, and the betrayal of confidence or expectation can be devastating. So whether or not the children are skyclad, you can say things like, "Well, we share our bodies with people we love and trust," and you should explain that sex is not the only way to share your body.

Hugging is sharing your body. Circling is sharing your body, because you hold hands in Circle *and* because the group's energy will enter into and flow through you. Pulling somebody out of a wreck or a swimming pool is sharing your body; police officers and

firefighters are sharing their bodies. Smiling at someone is sharing your body; so is carrying something for someone else. If you
include all of these sorts of things in your definition of sharing
bodies, then you've created a context in which Circling skyclad is
one of many acceptable ways to share your body with people you
love and trust.

Surrounded by grown-ups, and these days often inundated
by images confusing youth with adulthood, a lot of children's
feelings have to do with how *they're* doing with this growing up
business. When children find themselves inadequate, it's usually adult standards they can't meet. Again, it's important to
recognize your students' growth in its own terms, so that when
they're grown they can evaluate themselves in a wider context
and not depend, forever, on someone else's approval.

All the grown-ups in a child's life should express love and
approval. But this should not be the only praise children get
from parents and teachers, because with protective grown-ups is
not the only place our Witchlings will ever be. Ultimately, they'll
need to love and approve *themselves*.

Now You're Getting Bigger II

Be sensitive to opportunities to do a "getting bigger" Circle
for your older students. Start looking for those chances when
they're between the ages of 9 and 11 years old.

> Now you're getting very like
> The grown-ups that you know
> Let's go around the Circle
> And see what *deeper* Mysteries show.

As children get older and learn about their bodies—learn
that we're all carbon based and 98 percent water and that sort of
thing—they can understand that the Goddess and the God will
always love them because they are made from the same organic
material that makes everything, and that is the material body of
the Goddess Herself. The late Carl Sagan said that we are star
stuff, and he's right, in both senses. Everything that exists is

made of the same material in different proportion and relationship—us, red giants, white dwarfs, and the super-novas. Each one of us is unique, irreplaceable, and undeniably special and wonderful. Every one of us *is* a star, just as Aleister Crowley said!

The idea that we are conscious matter, with the capacity to guide our own lives as well as affect the rest of the world, is pretty amazing. Infants do not differentiate themselves from the world; younger children eventually come to differentiate their core family from the world; in later childhood and adolescence, children are still trying to understand the delicate balance there is between the inner and outer forces and being.

Their left brains are doing pretty well at this stage, and they tend to be (and will for the next few years) fairly linear-thinkers. They will appreciate teachers' efforts to explain things in Newtonian terms (to over-simplify a little). No matter how well older children can understand things with their left brains—the science and math classes they're taking might make at least some sense, and they may have certain rules and routines down pat—the right brain remains an adventure land for them for many years. Older children—even grown-ups—still need reassurances that they're fine, and they still need ways to remind themselves of this.

Spell Against Self-Doubt

Double, double, fear and doubt
Storms within and storms without
Let the tempest quiet be
So I can get in touch with me.

Double, double, calm and peace
Let the toil and trouble cease!
Let me find the place within
Where love and trust and growth begin.

With harm to none
My will be done.

Later childhood is a wonderful time to begin working more serious magic. Whether they make charms for their own goals or to express love for the world, older children's perception and motor skills are improved to the point where they can make simple pouches, and draw and fold simple talismans and amulets.

In your own Tradition, you will teach a particular style of charms and spells. You will take your students to the fabric store and show them what to use for pouches. Your students' needs and purposes will vary, but one thing most children could use anytime is a little magic help in discovering who they are. Here is an idea:

Identity Charm Spell

Draw a circle on white paper (notebook size is fine; unlined is better). Quarter it; in small letters around the outer circumference, label each space for one of the four Directions. With colored pencils, crayons, paints, or markers, draw a positive aspect (quality, characteristic) of yourself that relates to each Quarter. Do not use up the whole space with this drawing!

Next, draw things about yourself you'd like to make better, and put them in the Quarters where you decide they belong. When you're done, fold the circle inward so that it's square and none of the drawing shows. Hold it between your hands, straight out in front of you, and say:

> I am strong, and through the years,
> I will yet stronger come to be.
> Guide me, charm, through toil and fears
> to be the me I want to be.

Then, holding the charm tightly, think *very* hard about what you want to learn or change, and without letting go, say, "With harm to none, let it be done!" Seal your charm with wax, string, or a sticker you like. If you wear a pouch, put your charm in it while you're working on the things you want to make better. Otherwise, put it under your pillow or on your dresser where you'll see it or touch it every day.

Adolescence

Age

Adolescence (12-15 years old)

Developmental Needs/Work/Challenges

Peer relationships, the future, the community, self-consciousness, emotional intensity, physical changes; increasing responsibility.

Aspects of Wicca

Visualization, meditation, symbol and metaphor, more history, ethics, basic magic, simple invocation, Quarters, personal relationship to Goddess and God, personal use of magic and ritual, own Altar and Book of Shadows, study of Rede and Law, introduction to group work.

Well, here we are, face-to-face with one of the scariest Guardians there is: peer pressure. It can be heavy at times, and inspiring at others; turned against someone, it can also be devastating. One of the challenges adolescents face is to find more of their motivation and validation within themselves.

It's tempting for grown-ups to interpret teenage self-seeking as a rejection of adult or community values and concerns. It's also extremely patriarchal and authoritarian to look at it that way, and acting with extreme patriarchy, wielding power over each other, is something that Witches prefer to avoid. The problem is finding an alternative role model for parenting, mentoring, and teaching. Our solution is the approach we call **regency parenting**.

The next time you confront a child who will *not* take your advice, or will *not* follow your directions no matter how reasonable or angry you are, no matter how the child is punished or rewarded, remember this: **Whatever's on their minds must be very important if they're willing to take such a big risk for it.**

Risk? What risk?

The risk that you—parent, teacher, adult friend—won't love them any more, that they'll be turned away from the fire, into the jungle, onto the savannah, where they might die. That's a *pretty* big risk. It may not look like life and death to you, but it can feel like life and death to a teenager.

Even when we are fully mature, unconditional love is an issue. For someone whose body chemistry changes faster than a fashion model's clothes, assurance is fleeting. Teenage students may "know in their heads" that they're loved (accepted or respected) no matter what, but they aren't necessarily sure of it emotionally. What children "know in their heads" and what they learn changes as they progress through school and into the world, as well as challenges and remedies some of their childhood certainties. It will be some time before what teenagers know intellectually becomes a reliable resource for them.

This is one reason they become so intensely interested in specific and sometimes harsh rules. Instinctively, they're striving for order and balance. One challenge Craft parents and teachers face is to make sure students' ideas of order and balance aren't limited to opposition. As teachers, we have to make it clear, through experience and example, that balance involves cooperation, compromise, and lateral thinking as much as it involves "squaring off."

So, when a teenager _insists_ on something, take a hint. It doesn't mean you have to "give in." It means you have to acknowledge youngsters' feelings, perceptions, and passions. Teenagers understand that reality encompasses disappointment. They don't expect it to be all roses and no thorns. But a little back-rub after they've been bent double weeding all day wouldn't hurt; usually we're focused on telling them not to forget to wipe their feet or wash their hands and not to leave their muddy clothes on floor.

One thing we can teach teenagers, one tool we can bestow upon our students at this age, is how to approach the various relationships we make in our lives. One of those is the teacher-student (master-apprentice, in some cases) relationship. Teenagers are trying to distinguish themselves from their families, to establish their own identity in the community. If, as it may well be the case, you have known your students for years, it would be wise not to bring that long relationship too far into your "classroom."

We suggest slight distancing. You don't need distance between your and the student's interests and aptitudes, but you need to distinguish between the casualness of friendship, and the formality of the classroom. There are plenty of examples of this sort of thing, too, so we don't have to flounder around trying to gauge the appropriate distance.

Look at Merlin and Arthur: the wizard was devoted to the young king, but when teaching, he had to let the boy do his own work, no matter how much his uncle-ish nature might have moved him to ease the lesson. Distance doesn't mean insensitivity or ignorance, though. It means basing your relationship on the material you're teaching rather than on your personal relationship. The difference between you, "the teacher," and you, "the friend," might be difficult to define, but it will do you and your students a world of good. Especially in family covens, it's critical to distinguish between you, the parent or spouse or sister or brother, and you the teacher or Priest or Priestess. Teaching the distinction early will save time and energy later.

You need to be acquainted with the ways your students' minds work. Younger children make general rules in their heads, which derive from their own experiences. As their experience grows, physically and to take account of information from other people, as the volume of information and experience they have to integrate expands and threatens to overwhelm them, the rules they're formulating in their heads get more and more specific.

Teenagers are stepping back again to take into account a lot of new information as their own experience begins to widen significantly, and their understanding and application of indirect experience broadens and deepens. Relationships of all sorts generally occupy them almost entirely. Remember that relationships with teachers can get intense. Be ready to keep that distance, provide that balance.

Your students are trying to establish some workable standards: standards by which they can be successful and worthy; standards that will also define groups to which they can belong; and associations through which they can explore options, attitudes, and opportunities available to them.

They're asking questions like, "How do you know if you're *really* in love?" and "Can you give me $5?" In some ways, all these questions translate to, "Am I normal?" and "Will you always love me even if I'm not?" None of their questions should be ridiculed, even if they can hardly keep straight faces asking them; and we can't get mad about their jokes, even if we don't get the jokes or they make jokes all the time. ("Will you love me even if I bother you?")

Adolescent bodies are growing and changing as are adolescent emotions, responses, dreams, and ideals. It's unbalancing, which is why so many teenagers seem unbalanced, and why it's so impressive that so many of them manage to be such pleasant company anyway. With gym classes and dating pressures, body image can get awfully important, and telling them it "won't be so significant when you're older" won't help any more than it did when people said it to us.

The naked self is still buffeted by double standards in our culture. On the one hand, the curves, lines, colors, and textures of the body are used an awful lot in advertising. They are emphasized to varying degrees of taste on most television shows. On the other hand, people still worry that a little boy seeing his dad's penis will shame him and warp him for life, and people still think that a woman wearing specific fashions of the day is "asking for it." Nobody seems to be talking about the _other_ ways we can be naked before one another. My thesaurus offers synonyms for _naked_: bared, exposed, wide-open, plain, and frank. It's eye-opening.

No matter what you're wearing or not wearing, teenagers and adults can always benefit from a boost to their body image. The guided meditation that follows can be done alone, in a group exclusively female or male, and with people of nearly any age. (Recording it may challenge your "voice-image," too.)

Meditations such as The Mirror in the Meadow are meant to be heard by the person meditating. Commonly, we make audio tapes of someone else reading and including the appropriate pauses, or reading aloud and taping our own voices. A friend or working partner whose voice is soothing, and who can be attentive without intruding on the meditative experience can read in person. (Use a watch with a second-hand and make sure the pauses last 20 to 60 seconds.)

The Mirror in the Meadow

Before you start this (any) meditation, be sure there's a helping of your favorite fruit—a quartered apple, a fresh peach, grape juice—ready in the fridge or closer. If ever a guided meditation gets too heavy, stamp your feet (if you're sitting), or roll over (if you're on the floor). This will break the light trance and ground you. _Do not_ do extremely heavy work alone.

Pause at least 20 seconds, or much longer if you'd like, at each break (or paragraph change). Make yourself comfortable, in a chair or lying down. Breathe deeply to relax.

Imagine yourself stretching out on a blanket in a meadow. Enjoy the white fluffy clouds floating overhead. Inhale and let the smell of meadow grasses fill your awareness.

You can hear birds: mockingbirds, the cactus wrens, the grosbeaks. (Of course, you'll listen to the birds that live in your area.) You can feel the afternoon sun on your skin. You can feel the little puffs and breezes playing on the ground.

Now you feel yourself drawn toward the North. You stand up and in the North, you see a small hill, with a hedge at the top of it. You walk toward the hedge, slowly at first, but faster as you become sure there is something there for you.

You reach the top of the hill. The hedge is taller than you are, and circles the hilltop. But in front of you, there is a little arched doorway, and without any fear at all, you go through it. Inside, you feel entirely safe and comfortable. You see that you are in a hedge-maze, and you start walking, knowing that you will find the center.

Soon you find another arched doorway, and pass through it as well. You notice that you are very warm. You feel so safe that you take off your shirt, hanging it carefully on a branch of the hedge. You find another arch, and pass through it. You feel warmer still, and you take off your (pants, skirt), leaving (them, it) neatly folded at the base of the hedge.

Feeling velvety grass beneath your bare feet, you walk through another arch. Now you feel that you are very close to the center of the maze, and you are tingling with a pleasant anticipation. It is so warm now that you need no clothes at all, and so you take off whatever you're still wearing.

You notice, with no alarm, that for the first time, you are outdoors with no clothes on. You stop to feel the sun on your *whole* skin.

You notice the breezes differently now, too, and even the space around you feels different. Spreading your arms, you close your eyes and spin around until you fall, dizzy and delighted to the ground.

You're curious about the full-length antique mirror you see
in the dappled light under a tree in the meadow.

Under a tree, the light dappling its leaves, you are intrigued to see a mirror. It is an antique, full-length mirror. There is an image in the mirror, and you are curious about it. At first, all you can see in the mirror is a pair of feet, but they are beautiful feet, and you gaze at them.

Now you can see legs...now knees. You notice that their shape is perfect.

Now you see that the image in the mirror shares your gender. Looking at the figure's genitals, you feel no embarrassment or shame, only admiration for the beauty of the human body.

The figure's hips and waist are beautiful as well, and you begin to think this person must be holy.

You see the figure's chest now, formed in strength and beauty. You can see the figure breathing, and the steady rhythm is entrancing.

The shoulders, the arms, the hands...they are all graceful. The beauty of this figure makes you ache!

The throat, the neck, and now the face become visible in the mirror. At last the identity of this perfectly beautiful person will be revealed to you!

The face in the mirror...is yours. You realize that the entire body is yours. You look again. You are still beautiful. You realize that you have always been beautiful. You realize that your body feels beautiful. You are delighted, and you dance with your mirror image, laughing.

Suddenly you see that the tree sheltering you and your mirror bears your favorite fruit, and a ripe piece falls into your hand. It tastes wonderful, better than you've ever tasted before. You realize that seeing your own beauty has enhanced the taste. You realize that loving and delighting in your own body will enhance the rest of your life, too.

You finish your fruit, and it is time to go back. You move through the arches again, collecting your clothing as you go. Soon you are back at the entrance to the maze, and you can see your blanket at the bottom of the hill.

Full of freedom, you run as fast as you can down the hill. You never fall until you roll onto your blanket and relax.

When you get up, you notice another arch ahead of you, and you go through it. You know the center of the maze is not far from here. Through yet another arch you pass, and you are in the center of the maze. You look around. You notice the colors, the smells, the sounds. There are flowers and small trees, beehives and little den holes under the hedge. You notice them all, see what and who lives here.

When you have caught your breath and relaxed again, focus on your breath, and when you are ready, notice that you are back in your own time and place again. Go and have a piece of fruit or some juice, and forever remember how beautiful you are.

At the same time teenagers are working on getting comfortable with themselves, they're working on their relationships with other people. With relatively little experience in the world, and with their own identities feeling a little slippery yet, it's just plain *hard* for most teenagers to figure out how to act and what to feel. It is all too easy, though, for teenagers (and all children) to feel overwhelmed.

Mind you, most teenagers don't have a whole lot of trouble, and most parents can get by with being sympathetic rather than paranoid. Still, as a parent, teacher, or community Elder working with teenagers, you may run into some challenges. So? If all our talk about "strength in diversity" is to mean anything, mustn't we find strength in our children's differences from *us* as well? If all our professions to be non-hierarchical are sincere, then I think we must "disexpect" to have *power over* our children's lives.

The Adventure Tradition interprets obstacles or setbacks as challenges, those Elemental Tests heroes are always encountering on their Quests. Don't imagine for one minute that encountering weird apparitions and mortal perils is as glamorous as it looks in the movies! You'd have been riding all day in nasty, hot, dirty, and scratchy (not to mention stiff and stinky) leathers or cottons, on an old, tired horse. What you go through is every bit as challenging and significant; and so is what children go through.

The point is that you have committed yourself to a cause—to life, at least, for we believe that reincarnation is interactive, that we're here willingly—and one remains loyal to the Quest even when it seems hopeless or impossible. Honor, though ideas about it have ordered the rational world for centuries, is not measured by rational standards.

Neither is Wicca; neither is life. Our "worth" is that we are natives here on the planet, and natives of life, the universe, and everything. We don't have to "qualify" to be acceptable, not in this incarnation or any other. There is no lengthy or complex list of rules and prohibitions to cope with because, in Witch-craft, our instinctive behavior is largely proper to begin with.

Wiccans acknowledge two "rules." One is called the Wiccan Rede, the other's the Threefold Law. Neither commands us as much as *reminds* us of the facts of life.

The Wiccan Rede

"An ye harm none, do as ye will" could be the description of a natural law deduced from observation as well as a charge, a divine assignment. We have accepted the Rede as a *moral* obligation; yet it also seems to us that on the species level, it's a *biological* imperative: the more harm we do, the more comes to us. Studying the Rede brings up three major subjects to explore: the nature of *harm*, the scope of *none,* and the nature of *will.*

The Threefold Law tells us: "What you put into the Worlds returns to you threefold." In a class we attended once, a student asked how you could reconcile "threefold" with every action having an "equal and opposite" reaction. If we'd been teaching, we'd have answered that Newtonian laws apply only in certain realms of the physical dimension, and that what we do in the world has an effect on dimensions *beyond* the physical. It is from *those* dimensions that the other "folds" in the Threefold Law come. The point is that the behavior of our energy influences realms and dimensions we can't see, and realms and dimensions we can't see influence us.

It's pretty clear that with a Threefold Law literally and poetically in effect, what you put into the Worlds matters—and that's not a threat, it's a *promise*—that your efforts count, that you and your life changes the Worlds. The Threefold Law hints at Wicca's world-view; the Rede guides our behavior in the context of the Law.

The Rede is short and pithy, and not easily dismissed. Witches are not often comfortable with hard-and-fast rules; guidelines make more sense to us—and to children as well, providing they have some guidelines or techniques for interpreting the guidelines! Studying the Rede, which is likely to take several sessions, is very helpful for teenagers, who need both practice taking moral and ethical stands and getting feedback from mentors and peers.

Studying the Rede

Harm

Studying the Rede raises the question of defining "harm." Some harm we can do is obvious, but other harmful behaviors are less clear. Peer-group discussions are excellent forums for exploration of this and other concepts.

If you have anything along the lines of a chalkboard, a wipe-off board, or an easel with a pad of big paper and some markers, you can write down everybody's ideas without making many comments or judgments. Let the children make their own evaluations. In review, don't be afraid to "challenge" them gently—even if you agree with what they're saying—to *support* their opinions with personal experience, from books they've read, or with principles and ideas they've already learned from you.

Ideas of harm are different, not only from culture to culture, age to age, but from person to person and from time to time in one person's life. Understanding other perspectives helps define our own.

What can grown-ups contribute to these discussions?

- ✣ Ideas about how to tell whether something is harmful or not.

- ✣ Ideas about how to resolve conflicts over the definition of harm.

- ✣ Ideas about harm being differently defined for different species.

- ✣ Ideas about responsibility for harm done.

- ✣ Ideas about balancing harms and benefits.

To study other aspects of the Rede, here are more ideas. If you can, schedule at least an hour, more if you are working with more than six children, for each of these topics. Children will have their own questions and answers, and they will critique themselves as they go along.

If you need to nudge them at all, do so with questions or examples for them to consider, and not with any "right" answers in mind. The object here is to get them to learn how to think for themselves, and to trust their own reasoning on both sides of their brains.

None

Just who's included in the "none" we're allowed to harm? Students of the Rede need to consider this question.

- ✣ Are *you* included in the "none" you can harm?

- ✣ Does the Rede apply just to people you know personally?

- ✣ Does the Rede apply to other life forms? Which ones?

- ✣ Does the Rede apply to mountains, forests, seas, the atmosphere, and other elements of our ecosystem?

- ✣ Does the Rede apply only in the present, or to the future as well? What about the past?

As children become better able to coordinate their thoughts and feelings, their wills begin to develop. Their ability to do "formal" magic—work it deliberately, and be held responsible for it—is growing, and the issues encompassed by the Rede become more and more important.

The question of "will" is difficult to resolve for many adults; how much more complex it must seem to children, who have comparatively little experience, and whose passions are mercurial. It's a good idea to present several straightforward Craft opinions about the nature and use of will to children, and to let them participate in discussions. Their questions and interpretations will be different than ours, and may well shed some light on the subject for all of us.

Will

What is "will," anyway? Is what you *will* the same as what you *feel like* or *want*?

Will is discussed by many Wiccan, Pagan, and occult authors. Generally, it's thought that it's *not* just whatever you feel like doing, but more along the line of an inspiration or calling. Using the sources your Tradition draws on, make some excerpts available for the children to read and discuss.

Will is a difficult concept to thoroughly understand, and our ideas about it can change more than once. Because will is somewhat complex, certain aspects and qualities of it will interest us at different times in our lives and in our studies. This is not a subject you can wrap up in an hour, but one you and your students will come back to again and again.

Encourage teenagers to brainstorm about how to tell whether an idea for action is really a manifestation of will or just a mundane desire or convenience. Encourage them to use examples from their own lives.

Guilt Trips

Adolescent intensity applied to a study of the Rede and the Law can, encouraged by society's power-over structure, produce impressive guilt trips and deep angst. Rather than discouraging this by saying things like, "You're not responsible for all the woes of the world," encourage your students to turn that energy around and send it as far back into the world as it's gone deep in them. Suggest magic for inspiration and meditation on ways to right some wrongs, change things for the better.

This is what Witches do with energy, recycle it, rebalance it. Adolescents have plenty of energy, and they very much need to know ways to direct it and ground it. When adolescent Witches are feeling loathsome and despairing, for instance, they can blatantly lie on the Earth and sob all the guilt away, sending that great energy to Her to use as She requires.

Making commitments, and taking responsibility for them, is necessary and difficult for adolescents. Adults can understand in terms of our jobs: deadlines imposed upon us, the juggling we have to do to finish one project without letting others slide, the pressures we feel when there are changes in personnel or policy. It's like this most of the time for children, and we need to take their difficulties seriously even if the children know they don't have it as bad as they could. Their troubles are proportionately at least equal to ours, as their youth is proportionate to our adulthood.

Commitment is essential to successful magic. Okay, commitment is essential to successful just-about-anything. It's essential if our communities are going to last, going to survive change and challenge. And it's certainly essential if we're going to begin teaching our children. It's one thing for a family to raise their own children in the Craft, introduce them to the rituals they practice, explain things in their own family-Circle way. It's another thing altogether to offer what we call Sun Day School or Moon School classes. That requires even more time, energy, and money.

Commitment is difficult to teach; it must be modeled and encouraged over time. Think in terms of noticing the longer cycles, pointing out that you start making plans well in advance of festivals, etc. Here are a few other things to consider:

Making Commitments

How many times have you told yourself you'd do something, and then let it slip for weeks and weeks? How many times have you been frustrated when someone *else* says they'll take care of something and then they let it slide until it was too late or another person had to deal with it?

There are lots of jokes about "Pagan Standard Time" and *usually* we can grin and chuckle when somebody comes to a meeting late or arrives mid-way through a ritual—but when we really think about it, it can be downright annoying. Most communities deal with it by knowing who's likely to be late and either leaving that person outside the Circle if they come late, or designing rituals flexible enough to accommodate such habits. Many covens have a 15-minute rule: If you arrive later than that, you miss the ritual. We've all mused on how great it would be if things got started on time, and how well things would work if everybody remembered their own deadlines.

Being on time and keeping *other* commitments—writing an article for the newsletter, making phone calls to reserve the ritual site, finishing class assignments, attending to journal work, being sure the robes are ironed early—is something we can teach our children.

There are many reasons that people fail to keep the commitments they make. Sometimes there's an emergency, or an unexpected illness. Sometimes the job is bigger than it looked and too overwhelming to finish on time. Sometimes things just get away from us.

Ask your students to list the reasons *they* fail to keep commitments (of any kind). Then ask them to brainstorm about ways to keep commitments even when those reasons apply. Get them talking about how they feel when commitments made to them are not kept. Suggest that any commitment in a religious context (to keep a journal, to meditate daily, to make a banner for the next Festival, to provide the Cakes for the next Circle, etc.) is a commitment not only to the self and other people involved, but to the Goddess and God. Discuss the ways in which this commitment is different (if it is) from a commitment to other people.

Sometimes, a teen's life is going to seem like too much, and then, just as little children sometimes need "time outs" away from the over-stimulation of the world, adolescents need a break. Guided meditations are great for children. They're transporting, offering a relaxing break from routine and a safe escape from an often stressful mundane world.

Advantages of Guided Meditations

- Safe escape from mundane world.
- Establish habit of meditation time.
- Strengthen visualization skills.
- Develop concentration.
- Put in touch with inner strengths.
- Technique to access inner resources.
- Safe to share without risk of disease.
- Can be worked in spare moments.
- No expensive equipment is required.

It's Just Too Much

As for any "guided med," set out something to eat and drink afterwards, and make sure you won't be interrupted. Make yourself comfortable in a chair or lying on the floor. Take several deep breaths to clear your mind and relax your body. The narrator (another person or a tape of yourself) should pause at least 20 seconds between paragraphs, or as long as you'd like.

> You are in a deep forest. It is dark, but not frightening. Little bits of sunlight dance on the forest floor. Take a deep breath. Smell the trees and hear the birds. Feel the bark of the tree you're standing behind. Look around so you will know this place when you come to it again.

Off away to the North, you hear a sound. It is a faint sound, and it interests you because you can't quite place it. You start through the forest, following the sound. Parts of the path you find are easy. Parts are overgrown with brush, grasses, and young trees. The path gets more difficult to follow, but the sound gets louder, and you keep going.

After a hard walk, you reach a clearing. The sound you hear turns out to be the music of harps, and this is clear to you now though the harpers remain invisible. From the forest beyond, a tall, dark woman steps into the clearing. Notice what she is wearing, what she looks like, how she moves, so you will know her when you see her again.

She is carrying a large basket. She brings it toward you and sets it down in front of you. You both sit down. She introduces herself. Remember her name so you will know it when you hear it again.

She opens the basket and begins to take things from it. She lays them out on the ground in front of you. All of the things are dark and heavy looking, and you don't recognize any of them right away. As you look at them, though, you begin to see that they are symbols of your responsibilities.

There's a symbol for school, one for household chores. There's a symbol for all the jobs you have to do and all the expectations people have of you; there are others that you recognize, too.

When you recognize them, the woman pushes them all toward you. Then she brings out several more objects, and tells you that you must choose one more to add to the collection that is already yours. You are not sure what the new objects symbolize, but you know that you must choose one, and choose it soon.

You remember, while you are trying to decide, that you have seen sets of objects like this before. You realize that almost everybody has a set of responsibilities like this. Without being *entirely* sure what it represents, you choose one of the objects the lady offers. You thank her for it, even though you know it will mean more work for you.

A tall, dark woman carrying a basket steps from
the forest into the clearing.

She nods and tells you to work with the object for some time, and then to return to this place to talk to her about it. You agree to do this, and she stands and disappears back into the woods with her basket. The set of objects that symbolize all your responsibilities is before you, and you wonder how you can take them all back with you. You look around, and to the side of the clearing you see a tote bag with an amazing design on one side. Remember what it looks like, so you will know it when you see it again.

The bag is big enough to carry all the objects, and you pack them all into it, including the new one you have just chosen. Noticing that the bag is heavy, but not too heavy to carry, you make your way back through the woods to your special place. Pay attention to any birds or flowers or rocks you see along the way.

Back beside your tree, you sit down and close your eyes, wondering what your new responsibility will mean, and wondering what you will have to say to the Lady about it when you come back here. You can still hear the music of the harps, though it is very faint now.

When you open your eyes, you are back in your chair or on the floor. Take a few deep breaths. Remember as much as you can about this journey, and then make your journal entry and sketches.

If you are meeting regularly with a group of adolescents, you can use this meditation many times (with or without introducing new symbols or responsibilities). One of the developmental tasks adolescents face is *learning to integrate their experiences*. It is very easy for each event or circumstance in a teenager's life to be an isolated occurrence, and that makes it very hard for them to integrate their experience and see patterns.

Taking teenagers back to visit on a regular basis with Our Lady of Responsibilities (and learn more about their symbols and responsibilities) will help. In addition to expanding their personal relationship with the Goddess, it's an opportunity for them to think about the ways their responsibilities intertwine, support each other, and grow out of each other. If you have the facilities available, it would be a great idea for teens to use modeling clay to *make* those symbols of their responsibilities, and certainly it's a good afternoon's work to make drawings of the other designs that are given to them in this meditation.

The one caution you must observe here is not to *force* children to share their meditative secrets with one another, if they are at all reluctant to do so. In adult groups, to make the point that we *can* all trust each other, and that none of us is utterly alone in any thought or feeling, we often actively encourage sharing, but we must temper that enthusiasm with children.

Make it clear that whatever they share will be respected, and don't just tell them so, show them so in your behavior. Don't mock, and don't allow others to mock. Give students the freedom to grow into the perfect love and perfect trust we cherish so highly. They long for it, and they will come to it at their own pace. Just give them, as the God and Goddess have given all of us, space and time. As above, so below!

In school, adolescents are doing more and more writing; journaling is often an assignment. Not all Witches publish what they write, but all Witches write, from dream journals to ritual diaries, from volumes of poetry to research notes. It's good to encourage your students to start keeping journals. You may choose to give them their own Books of Shadows later, when they are young adults and ready or nearly ready for Initiation (if they're going that way). This, of course, is a decision that cannot be made unilaterally by one teacher, but must be reached by a consensus of the teachers and parents involved. In the meantime....

In our early teens, my friend Grianwydd and I had little three-ring binders, carefully covered with "beautiful" contact paper, which were called Magic Rings. These were gift notebooks, carefully decorated and begun with a poem or song or two, and grew to precious collections, written out by hand, of our favorite poems and songs.

Some of those songs were ones we wrote ourselves, so those Magic Rings were, in some sense, journals. Indeed, singing was so important to us that in a way, those Rings were Books of Shadows; we even kept them just as private. This is the poem that we kept—still keep—as the first page of our Magic Rings.

This is my Ring of Magic
My heart is tied within;
Leave these pages lying calm,
You, who would glance and grin.
Of when the stars would shine
Above the campfire's glow,
This book's soul sings with memories,
Stories and ballads hummed peacefully slow.
No matter whatever the years take and bring,
We are young who know secrets of Magic Ring.
This is my Ring of Magic,
Time has left it undimmed;
Throw down your load, please,
Stop awhile,
And pass with me within.

The one I have now is not the original, but Grianwydd's is; and my reconstructed (now covered in gold velvet) Ring came with us for years to every Sabbat and was shared around nearly every campfire until a new and more durable community songbook was required.

This Ring is a good and life-long friend in the same way a Book of Shadows is, and no less treasured; and it was easier to understand the nature of the Book of Shadows for knowing the Ring first. (Grianwydd reminds us of a difference between Rings and Books of Shadows: Rings can only be made for other people, and that *with* any Ring, a pair of drip candles *must* also be given, anointed for peace and protection.)

Children change so much between the ages of 11 and 15 years old that it might seem obvious that they're growing up. If we don't see them every day, their growth can seem quite startling. (I'm sure some children are a foot taller every time I see them!) It's not always obvious to them, though, and even if they do see it themselves, the community's recognition of growth at every stage is tremendously encouraging.

Here in the Southwest, there is an Hispanic tradition of introducing young women to society around her15th birthday, in a celebration-by-formal-dance called a Quincianera (pronounced *keencia-nerra*—quincé means 15 in Spanish). Even though boys aren't presented in any corresponding ritual that we know of, we still find it a wonderful idea. Indeed, coming-of-age rites are gaining in popularity, and while the Pagan teens who are "manned" or "womaned" are fairly few yet, we expect that in another decade, Manning and Womaning will be among the most common rites performed.

Think how proud—watch them shine right through their embarrassment—your students would be to be honored at a dinner. Think what it could mean to them—and to the community's younger children, and Elders—to hear from their parents and teachers and priestesses and priests how much they and their energy mean and matter to you.

An event of this nature conjures much of Wicca's heritage, with which teenagers need to connect, too. Remember that all of the Craft's ethnic groups met and meet in their own great halls or groves, around blazing fires, to trade stories and brag about skills. In some traditions (the Norse, for instance) those images are alive in Sumbels; in Druidism, Bardic Circles are held "all the time." For many Wiccans, it's the shadows of the old Celtic halls that flicker behind the candles in the living room.

These images and ideals of camaraderie are precious to us, and they are our children's and students' cultural rights, as well. We would serve Witchcraft and the Goddess and God well to bring those images and ideals to life for our children; and if their lives and their perceptions and perspectives are not worth our extra efforts, what on Earth is? Picnic or banquet, a gathering to break bread and pass the chalice in honor of your adolescents will enhance all your lives threefold!

Pass the Cup and Share the Bread

This is something between a toast and a blessing (there's a lot of overlap anyhow), and you can make it as casual or ceremonial, as private or public, as you feel is appropriate. Of course, you'll use the God and Goddess names common to your Tradition or community. If changing those names requires re-writing the rhyme, offer the effort to the Gods.

> We offer you the Pentacle
> We offer you the Cup
> We offer you our love and trust
> And we rejoice as you grow up.
> May the Watchtow'rs always bless you
> May you ever grow and learn
> May your hearts be brave and joyful
> Bless'd be by Cerridwen and Herne!

Young Adulthood

Age

Young Adulthood (16 years old and older)

Developmental Needs/Work/Challenges

Transition to adulthood, control of emotional energy, widening perspective and use of experience to make choices; introspection, testing values, and internalizing standards.

Aspects of Wicca

Initiation, own Tools, participation in adult ritual; coven membership; groups and gatherings; historical context; divination; composition of ritual; independent research and commitments.

The legal age of majority varies from state to state, and may be different for various social rights and privileges. The notion that you can get your driver's license when you're 16 years old used to be a constant; now it's 16 in some states, 17 or 18 in others. More and more states are opting to issue graduated licenses to young drivers, so their privileges increase as they demonstrate that they can handle the responsibility. Getting a driver's license is still a rite of passage for children in this country, and most teens look forward to it.

Other than drinking, which is legal at different ages in different states, driving is the great social passage in our culture. The following discussion is about driving, but the points it raises are relevant to other milestone events we can celebrate. But before we using driving as an example, I want to mention another, overlooked, passage event: registering to vote.

Wiccan lore tells us that social isolation once saved us, but today, it works against us. Wiccans need to be more active as *citizens* and need to see voting and other political activity as a kind of secular magic. Please encourage your children and students to register to vote. Encourage them—work it into your assignments whenever you can—to read a newspaper or watch the local news every day, so their votes will be well-informed. Think of voting as "civic magic," and prepare your students for working it. (Some of us are cynical, and don't vote because we think we can't make a difference, but what kind of example is that to show our children? One person can't make a difference? Then why bother doing magic?)

Driving, like voting, might seem utterly secular at first glance. But it has its magical aspects—even beyond the money and protection spells you'll probably feel like doing when your teens get behind the wheel. Certainly many a parent's first thought is of accidents and skyrocketing insurance rates, but look again!

Sure, the danger of accidents and the probability of rising insurance rates are real, but so are the *mythical* aspects of driving. To Witches and other Pagans, the mythical realms are as significant as the physical ones, but society pays very little conscious attention to them. Public culture focuses on driving as mythical in this sense: a sleek car is your ticket to sex. This is extremely superficial, but a group of friends driving to a party is not entirely dissimilar from a group of adventurers meeting at the inn and setting off on their adventures. Unfortunately, the forests of medieval legend were by all accounts *safer* than the "woods" our children wander today.

Apparently, most teenagers want to drive as soon as they can. They don't have to be going anywhere; driving, itself, is their destination. As parents and teachers, we can *fight* that (remember which buck usually wins, please) or we can "grow with the flow."

Before the Explorer was born, we owned a convertible MGB. Once or twice we entered ourselves in road rallies. We never won, but it was a real safe way to indulge that sheer love of driving that occasionally gets into us. There is absolutely no reason whatsoever not to organize a rally for (new) Pagan drivers. If there are a couple of teens who have just started driving, give everybody a break and give them a community-oriented, constructive way to vent that wonderful energy they hold. Think about assigning a certain amount of community work to your students. That might include offering rides to people who couldn't get to a meeting or Festival otherwise, taking the collective donation to the Food Bank, taking the local newsletter to the printer or to the Post Office, and volunteering to do other coven or community errands.

That would satisfy the energetic inclination to drive (to set out) while inspiring the care required in "assigned driving," and get some useful things done, too. Look out! It's a win-win solution!

Young adult energy can be directed to a number of tasks within the community, and it might be possible to agree to hire summer help and odd jobs from the adolescents and young adults among you. From asking them to help with the Spring purification or to help building a chest for the Tools, from hiring them to baby-sit, pet-sit, or house-sit, we can *all* offer lessons and opportunities to the teens following us.

Perhaps the most important gift we can give is a safe environment to grow up in. Part of "safe" is the provision of basic needs, and in an environment, that means a place—ground and community—where children can do what they need to do to grow up. We're fortunate to be part of a "camping contingent" that gets together for a few Sabbats every year. Our group members' ages range (so far) from 2-ish to 55-ish. It's great for the children, it's great for their parents, and it's great for those who aren't around "kid energy" very often. We're all family at camp, and the children respond to, and energize, all of us. We are, proudly, one of the villages it takes to raise children.

Children of every age need safe space; young adults need to practice various adult roles and skills. They need to be safe while they quest into their minds. They need us to be a "place" where they can flounder about, messing things up the first few times they try, where even if they make a really bad mistake, and even if they meant to when they did, they don't face execution *or* excommunication.

It comes naturally to children at any age to express themselves physically, and to follow cycles of solitary, group, and intimate activity. Young adults have a great deal of energy, and they're coming up with their own ideas of how to direct it, too. (Try sports events, and variations on the old shirts and skins games. Limber up and join them. And please don't say "I hate sports." Remember, the Olympics are Pagan!)

It will do no good to challenge children's power now, and could do a great deal of harm. They *are* strong and powerful, and it is their proper instinct to challenge the world. Unfortunately, however, the tendency of our mainstream culture is to squelch this exuberance.

A lively, multi-generational ritual in the woods puts us
in a festive mood and strengthens our sense of community.

Shouldn't Witches, workers of energy that we are, *benders* and *shapers* that we are, try to direct it constructively? We think so. We must look at the coming generations—all of them—as resources to be cherished and nurtured.

The War Against Children

In the 1980s, while corporate raiders leveraged (borrowed) their way to great personal wealth and social prestige, envious and obviously confused citizens supported draconian cuts in public investment. We're still feeling the effects of those and similar, ongoing efforts. Children, among the least able in our society to assert their claims to a piece of the budget pie, have suffered disproportionately.

At every turn, the very things they need most are withdrawn from them. Education budgets at every level have been cut: teacher salaries stagnate, equipment and texts become hopelessly outdated, class sizes increase, curriculum choices disappear—sports, music, and art programs are the first to go. Test scores are more important than teaching. Outside our schools, other "frills" eliminated or reduced by our conscientious budget-cutters have been equally devastating to the young. Public housing, children's health care, daycare funding, parental leave, after-school programs, and summer jobs have all been sacrificed to the orthodoxy of conservative economic policy.

Consequently, our courts have become crowded with dysfunctional teenagers. Perversely, they face a system of justice pressured by a fearful public to try them as adults, and to claim that an abusive up-bringing is not mitigating.

Across the country, Witches and other Pagans are in custody battles with their families and with public agencies. Why? Sometimes it seems like the answer to that question is that we're too *good* to our children. We won't teach them to accept force as authority, we won't teach them to respect or fear law-enforcers (real or "supernatural") who are, themselves, outside the law.

As above, so below; as in the past, so today: we're still in trouble because we're in the way of somebody's total dominion.

We must be very careful not to compromise our position toward power-over when dealing with young adults. They need to be able to feel that we are all Companions on the same Quest. Power-with respects their decision-making even if the consequences might be worrisome.

Young adults are very conscious of the behavior of adulthood, and often expect to be accorded all the rights and privileges at once. Sometimes, that's more than they bargained for. Because they are still very vulnerable of ego and heart, still not all that firmly established as distinct and authoritative personalities, we have to be careful how we help them.

When a decision has been made, even if it is not one you would make, barring immanent mortal peril or disaster, you probably have to accept it. If you feel that it is a dangerous decision, talk to your child. When you present objections, expect them to be countered. Allow for the possibility that your objections will be *adequately* countered, and that you might be able to change your mind. That's not giving in, that's being reasonable. It's what you want your children to do, and you have to show them how.

Most Wiccan parents do magic for their children. Protective magic, usually, and health and success magic. If something your child is doing scares you but not enough to forbid it, it's okay to do some magic over the whole thing to keep your child safe. However...

However, it is **unethical** to do magic for anyone without their permission, and what you need to do, in individual cases, is present your concern and the magic that you propose to do. Say something such as, "You are firm in this decision that you have a right to make, and I accept that. I am worried, though, about this possibility...." Explain what worries you calmly and matter-of-factly. Then say something such as, "I can't live your life for you and I can't keep you from all danger. But with your permission, I will (cast this spell, work this magic, make this charm) to give you what protection I can."

This example lets young adults know that you are respecting their individuality and their right to make their own decisions. It *also* lets them know that there are serious decisions that *will* have repercussions they may not have predicted or considered. It shares your concerns explicitly and acknowledges that no one else can, and you do not presume to, have complete power over their life.

Asking permission to do magic for your children—and honoring their authority to give it or not—is also a living lesson in Wiccan ethics. As our children become capable of taking responsibility for themselves, we must make sure they have a corresponding awareness of their own authority. The Goddess lets us know, in Her Charge, that She expects to see both power and compassion, both honor and humility in each of us. The Threefold Law also prompts us to treat our children with respect for the unique individuals they are. If respect is what you want from them, for you and the world, then respect is what you must show them.

Does this mean we can't do magic for our children when they're too young to give us permission? No. It means that when they get old enough to make decisions for themselves, we shouldn't sabotage their decisions with our magic, and we shouldn't manipulate children behind their backs. If you're going to do magic on them, do them the courtesy of letting them know (and realize that if you do it over their objections, you're putting yourself, magic, and Wicca, in a bad light).

You still have plenty of authority in their lives, and if you're going to demand that they do something, or forbid them to do something else, then do so from your parental authority, not in some sneaky, back-handed manner. What you put into the Worlds comes back to you, and if you set a standard of deception, your kid will do his or her best to meet it.

Sometimes, though, we're as respectful, as patient, as tolerant, as honest—as "good"—as we can be, and still it seems we're getting only "bad" back for our efforts. Though young adults can understand complex explanations of the idea of "karma," they need as much as little children to be reassured about how it works. (We used to distinguish, for the Explorer, between "something you did wrong" and "something that happened to you." There is no "you're a rotten scumhead" category.)

In fact, children wrestle with the concept of karma (at its broadest) their whole lives. It's not at all uncommon for youngsters to blame themselves for everything that happens in their family—and many readers of this book will remember how uncomfortable that unspoken guilt made them feel. Too few children understand the differences between "responsibility" (often glossed as response-ability) and blame or guilt.

You might hear people speak glibly of their own karma and the damage they laughingly admit doing to it. It's a Sanskrit word, "karma," and the concept comes to us through Hindu and Buddhist cultures most of us are not familiar with. But while most Westerners don't have the cultural experience to understand *karma* the way Hindus do, Wiccans, at least, have our own karmic understanding: that what we offer to the world comes back to us and contributes to the constant recreation of the worlds.

One karmic well-meant affirmation the New Age makes is that we all create our own reality. I want to say right off that—and this is true even if we smoke or drink or eat too much! **We do not individually create our own injuries and diseases.** Sure, there's social responsibility—keep voting, keep writing your representatives about the pollution in your area, etc. We have a responsibility to participate in our own healing—watch the diet, exercise, use sunscreen. But if you have breast cancer or heart disease, or if something else awful has happened to you, it's not because "you asked for it." Such accusations come from the premise that victims are responsible for their own injuries, and that's just, how shall I say it? Ignorant, cruel, and altogether too "con-veeeen-ient" for those in power-over.

There is not one of us who is the only person in the world, and what we do doesn't bounce back to us unchanged by the other energy it has encountered. Wicca does not subscribe to the theory that beauty equals "goodness" and ugly equals "evil," or that the mistakes we make are the manifestations of the unworthiness of our souls. Those are Puritan ideas, but they have so taken over our conscious minds that we forget that they reflect a religious attitude. They don't reflect Wicca's attitude.

The way we create our own realities is close to the way we prune roses. We step back far enough to see the rosebush's potential and get rid of the branches not working toward it, so the rose can give its growing energy to the branches that *do* work. But it's not under a gardener's control where the branches are originally. The gardener can't guarantee that every plant will be healthy—the gardener can't even be sure until it's opened that the nursery has sent the right plant! In our gardens, we have no control over the weather, the neighbors' animals, or roving garden vandals. We can do *something* about how those roses turn out, but not everything. Does that mean it's not worth growing roses? It does not!

Any system of "karma" is a reassurance that what we do in this life matters to the universe. Wiccans find that reassurance in the Threefold Law. (No, it's not just a threat!) The Western vague understanding tends to be that if you're bad in this life, you'll come back as something horrible and lowlier in the hierarchical ranks of species, and if you're really good in this life, you can either come back as somebody rich and popular, or not have to come back at all. Well, gosh!

Let's dispose of this "not have to come back at all" part first. Think about this: We dance the Spiral Dance, we die, we are reborn—and if being incarnate was a *bad* thing, then *nothing* would be reborn, would it? We'd all die and go back to the Mother, go from Individuality to Wholeness and *stay* there, and there'd be no material world at all. So when you wake up and you're still here, and the world is still here around you, you've just had Her assurance that life itself (including you) is good and holy and pleasing to Her. The Dance itself is sacred—both poles, life and death, and the passage back and forth between them. There's the Wiccan trinity: Goddess, God, and Their dance, *the* Dance.

We have our Threefold Law assuring us that what we do in the world really matters, even beyond our perception. We have the Wiccan Rede, "An ye harm none, do as ye will," reaffirming that it is possible to do as we will without anybody getting hurt. The liturgical material most Wiccan Traditions hold in common points to a very different concept of "karma" than most people understand. Take time to explore "the whole notion" with your children.

It's easier to let your teenage students (or sons or daughters) know that magic *is* for use in your whole life, not just in Circle, when they're reasonably well-grounded in the "mechanics" of Wiccan ethics. It also sets a good example. Even in psychic families, it's not fair to hold people responsible, emotionally or practically, for things you haven't actually *told* them. If you want you children to understand Wicca the way you do, then you need to make your understanding clear. Talk to young adults about Wicca and how you interpret it, how you practice it, and why—in as much depth as they can handle.

Reevaluate often how much they can handle. This ongoing involvement lets them know your relationship with them (and theirs with you and with the world) exists on many levels, and it reassures them of their worth and power on many levels. If there are several young adults in your community, then group discussions of parental experience and concerns and youths' expectations and intentions might be possible. These could be workshops, part of a weekend's getaway.

The Retreat

For years the Pagan community has enjoyed a number of retreats, workshops, and Festivals. Though older children and adolescents will enjoy "Witch Camp," the young adults have the most immediate gains to make, especially from retreats.

A weekend's retreat—sleep-over with workshops—might begin on Friday night with chanting and drumming Opening Circle, and continue with two or more workshops on Saturday, a Blessing Circle at noon, more workshops to follow, and chants after dinner, these while moving around the room or property. Sunday morning participants can move into small groups, maybe to talk more about workshop material, maybe to design elements of the Closing Circle. Your community's circumstances and resources will offer other possibilities and inspire other ideas.

"Out in the woods" will strike many as the traditional, and thus ideal, site for such a coming-together. We think so, too; but it'll work just as well in somebody's big backyard if you can spend a night or two crashed in sleeping bags on the ground.

To gather the young adults of a community (their ages ranging between 16 and 22 years) to acknowledge that, now, their own adventures will be calling them is enormously empowering for everyone. Children need ritual assurance that their parents and the community Elders will honor them as they "follow their bliss," as Campbell would say. They'll have our examples of Wicca's cultural and religious concepts for norms. With these life-shaping "Tools" available, they'll be *much* less likely to get in trouble trying to find a context in which they can honor themselves.

Our parents were horrified by some of the things we did; even when time has proved our decisions *not* to be mistaken or foolish, some of us still receive no acknowledgment from our

On a retreat in the woods, physical comfort is directly related to camp-work you do.

parents. That can be painful. We can heal ourselves, though, and we can decline to inflict that pain on our children or students. Do this by acknowledging that we make mistakes too, and that we learn from them, and so will our children. When we told our parents, and when our children tell us, "C'mon, you guys, it's my life!" it's true.

Those of us who *have* heard our parents say that we are really grown-up now, and that they're proud of us even if they don't agree with everything we say and do, know that it feels *good*. Is there any reason our children and our students should not hear that from *us*? (All acts of love and pleasure are Her rituals; She asks naught of sacrifice.) Helping our students broaden their perspectives forces us to broaden ours. This is one of the many mysterious ways in which the Goddess and God work.

A Toast and Blessing for Young Adults

Whether it is part of a larger Circle or other event or not, this toast should begin with a blessing of the wine by a priestess and priest, preferably in full regalia (no matter what everybody else is wearing). The Toast is given before the cup is given to the priestess, the Blessing is given before it is passed around.

The Toast

To the young and strong among us,
To the passion in their breasts
To the Wonders they'll encounter!
To their taking of the Tests!
To their pride and flying colors,
To their doing what they must:
They are masters of their destinies
Yet forever part of us.

The Blessing

Vision of East guide you,
Heart of South bide you,
Womb of West tide you,
Strength of North hide you.
Much may you learn
From Diana and Herne;
Rich stories may you share
When next we gather here.
Blessed be; in peace and safety go.

Another way of widening young adults' perspectives, of providing them with a wider context than the family's or the local community's in which to evaluate their understanding of themselves and the world, is at any of the big Gatherings.

The sky looked threatening: the Explorer gets ready to help Canyondancer string a tarp over the community table.

At big Gatherings, where people meet who don't already know each other, everybody's personal authority is taken for granted (in the good way). People speak respectfully to each other, people make sure not to step on or bump into short folks (two- and four-legged). People tell stories and share songs, experiences, opinions, and ideas. Those wonderful friendly arguments erupt everywhere. The kind of conversation you come away from feeling refreshed and with something to think about.

There are late nights and snack forays, spontaneous workshops and demonstrations. There are flare-ups of rudeness and tact, bushy-tailed energy and exhaustion. There are costumes galore, and few inhibitions. A Gathering can give young adults a sense of our genuine appreciation of diversity, and of the vastness and depth of the nation-wide Pagan community they belong to.

As overused and clichéd as it may be, it's important for young adults to "find themselves. Finding yourself implies you are someone and somewhere—that you live in a world, not in a vacuum. It seems to many Witches that the bigger the world you find yourself *in*, the bigger *you* can be.

Some people see it another way: the only way you can be "big" is to *look* big against a very small background. Witches tend to disagree with that. It may be true enough in the Newtonian sense, and it *is* what allows us to take vacation photos of ourselves holding up buildings or holding someone else on the palms of our hands. In the complementary magical realms, the polarities are reversed, and the reasoning goes more like this: giants can't be a proper giants in very small places because they have to hunch over to fit. Our students need big places to grow big in, and one of the first places we all should learn to *make* bigger is our *hearts.*

Another way of putting it is this: Much little like koi growing as big as the pond will let them, children will expand to explore all the possibilities they're aware of. Our job as teachers of Wicca is not so much to make them aware of the "right" possibilities (although we'll certainly teach them our Traditions) as it is to make them aware that the possibilities are infinite. There are good paths other than the "straight and narrow," and there are destinations other than the "top of the ladder." That's the sort of thing we need to make clear to them.

If they accept the idea that we're strengthened by diversity as a fact of life, they won't be deceived or coerced by anyone preaching any "only true ways." They'll all choose their own ways and maybe find new ways! As long as they're able to choose from a wide range of choices, we can trust that they'll (sooner or later) make the right choices for themselves, and we can trust them to learn from their mistakes (unless we let them misunderstand that mistakes invalidate effort).

Our children don't often just step out the door with their stuff in a backpack anymore, though for eons young adults pretty much did. The idea that courteous behavior, a pure heart, and so forth will win you through has probably been eyed skeptically for several centuries. There are more brigands and evil wizards out there to prey on our children than there were for some of our forebears and some of us.

Still, go they will (and must) and we must be aware of this and prepared to accept it. Part of our jobs as regents (parents or teachers) is to give our blessing to their enterprises and their efforts to master various skills. Driving is one of them, and it's an initiatory experience children share in most Western cultures. Though it's meaningful literally, the following discussion is a template for the similar attention we should pay to other meaningful milestones in our children's lives.

We know our children will leave. Our concern that they go in *safety* gets deeper and wider once they can drive. The process of getting a driver's license is nerve-wracking, and raises lots of energy in children and parents. To consolidate and ground some of that energy, a driver's blessing follows! Remember that though it is a driver's blessing, with very few changes it can become the blessing of other milestone achievements and endeavors as your sons and daughters take more and more responsibility for themselves.

A Young Driver's Blessing

> May the attention of the East be with you,
> that your vision be clear and wide.
> May the spirit of the South be with you,
> that you know when to exercise caution.
> May the tides of the West be with you,
> that you understand the depth of this responsibility.
> May the strength of North be with you,
> that your body be responsive and safely kept.

In the Old Days, the secrets of traveling were given only to an Initiate. Now, people who have no idea of the Mysteries, or how to penetrate them, are traveling far and wide (and blindly), without thinking of the responsibility they have accepted.

Earning your driver's license is a significant achievement, and we are proud of you. We understand this as a passage, and in our eyes,

when you take the keys to the car, you are accepting responsibility for
the Rede and the Law. Driving is action:

an ye harm none, do as ye will.

Go in peace (and not over the speed limit). Blesséd be.

The other sort of magic you're working here is the magic of
letting your teenagers know you're aware of them as individuals
and in tune with what's important in thier lives. Feeling grown-
up is very important to children sixteen and older. Their bodies
seem grown (although there may be more height or girth to come)
and now they're just about legal—they can't drink and they can't
vote, but they can drive, shop and, in some states, they can get
married. Their bodies are urging them to do all these things, and
more. They want to be treated as adults, but they don't quite
have an emotional handle on being grown-up.

We need to be sensitive to this in our children. Yes, they will
sometimes be as goofy as two-year-olds (Lord love 'em), and sometimes seriously obnoxious (Lord love 'em even more). They need
to know—and we need an occasional reminder—that for all their
multi-directional energy, we *do love* them and they *are* part of the
clan. They're on the verge of heading out on their own, and that
makes it particularly important for them to know they have some
place to come from.

Be alert to opportunities to ritualize acceptance of your young
adult into circles wider than your immediate family: your coven
(outer court, perhaps), your clan, your philosophy, the wider world
of Paganism, etc. Make these and other safe but non-ordinary situations part of your child's life. They need the experience of social
situations where they are successful just by being who they are.
Meeting the Quarters and the Gods is one situation where *who we
are* is all we need to be.

Ritual (re)introduction to the Gods and the Elements can
take much the same form as it does for younger children. Indeed, it
should take a similar form to any previous Passage rites and the
gifts that the Quarters offer now might be the same light-hearted

symbols you've used at other ages. But they might be more sophisticated, particularly if you know a young adult is working toward Initiation. If one or more of these gifts is relevant to some future plan, so much the better.

At this stage, you might like to use your child's formal name or a Craft name, if he or she has chosen one yet. You might also like to provide a special box (you can find them at thrift shops and in Craft stores and catalogues, and if you want to finish it yourself or let your child prepare it, you can look in "small-c" craft stores) in which your child can keep his gifts.

If you have not gone into Naming with your students, consider presenting some information in a workshop, in which they can focus on some experience likely to inspire names. You don't have to make it an away retreat, either. Put some blankets and hangings on the walls, pull the shades, light candles, play appropriate music, dress specially, eat specially, and work intensely. Naming is power.

Now You're Getting Bigger III

> You've come of age, my lovely child.
> You're both beguiling and beguiled.
> No one must carry you or hold your hand;
> Well done and welcome to our merry band!

If a Book of Shadows is Significant in your Tradition, then you'll need to think in terms of the young adults entering it having a Book of Shadows of their own. The dominant images of Books of Shadows are from Disney cartoons and Hollywood's B movies (the horror flicks). Those leave the impression of one huge book that contains every piece of knowledge available.

In the real world of real Witchcraft, though, many modern Witches have more than one BOS. There are formal and informal books, bound and loose-leaf; there are whole Books containing nothing but spells, rituals, dreams, or poems. The idea that when they reach a certain point, things will stop changing and be written down once and for all is not our idea!

Even if your students know that they'll have different ideas over the next several years, that their attitudes and preferences aren't consolidated yet, get them their own Book of Shadows. (Perhaps we should say, *especially* if you know they'll be exploring many different perspectives. After all, what we put in our BOS we must consider sacred, and "sacred" is a good way to look at growth.)

Presenting a Book of Shadows could be part of a Dedication or Initiation, or part of an Acknowledgment of Adulthood. (An Acknowledgment may or may not be part of a rite celebrating signs of sexual maturity, as most of us mature sexually well before we're really adult.) Whether to give a BOS privately or publicly, whether to inscribe the cover or leave that to its owner are questions of custom and style that must be decided by the presenters. In different communities, under different circumstances, the details of such rites must be appropriate to the people participating.

Your First Book of Shadows

A Book of Shadows is a big deal. Most of us have ours for many years, and refer to them often. Our Books of Shadows are *meant* to grow as we do. What you write today and what you write tomorrow, next year, and 10 years from now will be different. This is as it should be; but in the meantime, you want it to be perfect, and maybe you're not sure how to arrange it or even whether your handwriting is nice enough for it. Here are some ideas that might be useful:

- Make notes and sketches on scratch paper first to see how various pages might work.
- Enter the first things you learned in the first pages of your BOS.
- Enter what you think is the most important thing you've learned in the first pages of your BOS.
- Leave the first page of your BOS blank.
- Mark a section for recording your dreams.
- Illustrate your book.

A Book of Shadows with unlined pages looks nice, but few of us can write straight across the page without lines. I make "invisible" lines in mine with a sheet of dark-lined paper, a ruler, and the back-side of a table knife or crochet hook, to trace the lines. Laying the lined paper over the blank page and with the ruler laid along them,

Most Wiccans have more than one Book of Shadows
left to right, Campsight's reference volume, formal Shadows, and working BOS.

trace the lines with the blunt edge of the tool. This leaves two or three pages below the lined sheet lined with indentations that will eventually disappear. You can mark your margin and illustration lines this way, too.

The invisible lines on the page of the BOS aren't the only invisible forces influencing older children and young adults. Their hormones are invisible, too—but they don't help us stick to the "straight and narrow." Young adults need to ground the energy of their hormones. They also need to feel victorious. It used to be that they could satisfy both needs by participating in hunts, undertaking other physical challenges including bearing children, by serving the tribe in some significant way. These creative outlets are less and less available for children today, although it's easy to get in trouble in an attempt to meet the same needs.

We may not be able to change the whole of society overnight even with our most powerful and exhausting magics; but we can turn some things around for our students. Whether their challenges are individual or a team activity, children who are legitimately challenged, who can achieve meaningful victories, will not be tempted to take foolish risks. (We can't stop them from taking risks, but we can encourage them to take worthwhile ones.)

Even the smallest Pagan community can create a challenging environment for its young adults: One year, record-low temperatures gave the Tucson Area Wiccan-Pagan Network a record-low turn-out at their annual Yule caroling (through the Christmas-lights Neighborhood). So, the board recommended renting a hay-wagon the following year. That's an experience not many children have these days, but through one community's effort, a few city Pagans will know the touch of the wagon's worn wood, the rhythm and sound of wheels behind a horse. For some, it may be the first experience of a horse's breath on a cold night! That hour-long experience will be one they can call up from memory, even if they never get close to another wagon or another horse again. It will forever enrich them, no matter how subtly.

Whether you or your community take your children on a wagon ride like TAWN's, take them camping, train them in dance or martial arts so they can make those semi-annual sword fights more real, or engage them in civic projects, giving them these sorts of experiences gives them their best chance at hearing—and answering—their calls. Giving them these sorts of experiences is our responsibility, if we're parenting and teaching as regents.

Now, the Pagan community in Tucson is fairly large, and is composed of many traditions. For several of the Festivals, there are plenty of options: There's a now-independent "camping contingent," there's a group at the University, and there are other groups that share their hearths and acres. I don't like having to choose among events, but there's strength in diversity, and I sure do appreciate having a choice. (The root of our word *heresy,* by the way, is Greek, and means *choice.*)

We gather at "second Sunday cauldron-lucks" in a local park. The Tucson Area Wiccan-Pagan Network has been meeting for over 15 years now. The Explorer used to come with us sometimes, but eventually he chose not to. It would have been easy to feel that his choice to stay home, or to go somewhere else in the meantime, was a rejection of Wicca, a rejection of our Circles and circles of friends, a rejection of us. It would have been easy because that's the example our parents set. But it would have been wrong, because that's not how life really is.

Life is far more complex than that! It's not a grid of either-or intersections, it's a three-dimensional web that's always being spun. You don't have to go down any strands you don't want to, but it's absurd to think of trying to destroy or slander all the strands except the ones you use. Difficult to comprehend as some find it, and as vigorously *denied* as it is, the fact is that if you cut somebody else's strand of the web, your own is weakened.

Plenty of parents and teachers know how horrible it feels to be emotionally "dissed," yet startlingly often, we tell our children that they *don't* believe what they've just said they believe, or that they *don't* feel the way they know they do. "You don't really mean that! You don't really feel that way!" How many times did someone say it to you? How many times will your children or students hear it from you? Better to tell them (and believe) that they have a right to their feelings, and a right to claim their energy and live bound *only* by the Rede and the Law (not that saying "only" means it's easy).

We all know, from experience, that people get scared when they're isolated. That's why children who are shut out of the culture's social structures tend to band together in gangs: to get as close as they can to a sense of belonging and worth. That's why prisons isolate particularly troublesome inmates in solitary confinement, to diminish their sense of belonging and worth. It's the lurking danger under the cultural obsession to be entirely self-sufficient. It goes a long way in explaining why people lie and cheat on the Internet, in a badly twisted grab for acceptance.

Knowing that they are bound by the Rede and the Law gives young adults the security of a matrix in which their thoughts and feelings and behavior make a difference. It reminds them that there are other people to whom they matter and who matter to them. Whether or not the young adults in your community are aiming toward Initiation, this is a good time to let them in on your Tradition's Big Picture, and the even bigger picture of Neo-Paganism. Most of us use several metaphors to explain the structure and meaning of the world, and most of us have favorites. Now that the students are just about to graduate, it's time to share those favorites with them, and let them know *why* they are so meaningful to us.

This does not mean letting them in on Initiatory secrets before their time. This means sharing *personal* experience with them. It means telling them stories about your life, about the way the Craft has changed you and blessed you and nourished you. You may have shared these things, some of them, with your *own* children, but remember that, to other people's children, you may be one of the community's Elders, with an obligation to make your wisdom available to them, too.

Okay, you may not be able to get away with calling it "wisdom" unless the children in your community are tactful beyond their years. Whatever it is, you need to share it with them, consciously; for you are always sharing it with them, but not always consciously. We let our children know, in lots of ways, how we think and feel about things, and it's okay to convey some things unconsciously: learning a preference for pink geraniums from the planter outside Grammy's kitchen window is fine. But there are other things we need to share—teach—more attentively.

Religion and Politics

It may happen that one day, maybe after a civics class, that your child wants to know how your Wiccan faith affects your political positions. We have to be careful of these questions. Not because there's only one correct "Wiccan" political position, but because it's so easy to imply that there is! Wicca, many of us say, "is about personal responsibility." This is a good time to talk about voting and the responsibility of citizens to have a clue what's going on in the world, just as you make proper preparations for your spells and Sabbats.

Pagan opinions span the political spectrum, and we sometimes change our minds and take new positions when we come across new information about the issue. This is as it should be, for knowledge, after all, is power. In addition to developing an interest in local and national news and the issues that confront us as citizens, our children need to know, from us, a little bit about the issues that concern Neo-Pagans. Across the board, they need to know that while squabbles sometimes get the "headlines," there's more quiet cooperation, nation-wide, than there are local tantrums.

Your own political allegiances are probably guided by your interpretation of Wicca or another Neo-Pagan faith. Whatever relationship there is between them is what you should share with your children, when they ask. (If you haven't explored the relationship between your religion and your politics, do it!) There's no one right way to bring religion to meet politics, and there are lots of different ways to talk to your children about your own politics. Show them your decision-making process not to convince them of your position, but as an example of *how* mundane choices are made in consideration of faith. They need to know not only that not every Wiccan feels or thinks the same way you do about domestic or international issues. *Most* especially, they need to know that you love them even if they *don't* feel or think the same way you do about things.

Coming from the Adventure Tradition as we do, Canyondancer and I think the ideal place to have those deep discussions, and to tell important stories, is around a campfire. This is not practical for everyone, but there are other ways to achieve a similar effect.

Times are so different from when "boomer Witches" were coming of age, that it's sometimes hard to see how our youthful experiences are relevant to the lives our children lead now. If, however, you can tell stories in the dark, around a fire, you can achieve a sense of timelessness in which the differently detailed stories can illustrate the same enduring themes of human life. At this level, whether you're in the woods, in front of a fireplace, or around votives on the living room floor, stories become symbolic, therefore "translatable," and thus relevant to *any* age and culture. The medium is as important, in its own way, and as impressive as the message. Not only can you communicate to your students a little more easily in these circumstances, but you also forge a bond through your shared light-trance experiences.

Back to the Caves

When you are ready to sit down around dancing flames and tell your stories, begin with a few group breaths or a chant to relax and synchronize everyone. Hold hands and say:

> Body to body, mind to mind
> Above, below, before, behind
> Culture to culture, time to time
> Heart to heart, mundane, sublime
> We are the spiders, we are the threads.
> We are the Witches, back from the dead.
> Weaving our stories, weaving our spells,
> Past, present, future: the One Story tells.

If you are teaching a class, it may be appropriate to celebrate a Graduation. If your students are young, you'll need to prepare it for them; if they are older children, they can contribute something, help plan the event. Adolescents and young adults may want to contribute a little or a lot, depending on the sense you've given them of Craft etiquette and what to expect of people and rituals! (I hope the *Harry Potter* movies have given new impetus to the use of wizard's caps for mortar-boards.)

Assuming your students pass their tests to your satisfaction, you'll want to commemorate this and acknowledge their learning. You can make wonderful certificates on the computer, or you can make them by hand—it might depend on how many you need! A bit of sealing wax, or maybe a frame, makes a nice finishing touch.

If they're older, some of your students are probably considering Initiation or an Initiatory path. For those who are sincere, but realistically too young for such a step, consider whether a Self-Dedication might be appropriate. Self-Dedications do not have to be solitary affairs, either. A devotee can have helpers, witnesses and well-wishers, and a Self-Dedication is as much a reason to celebrate as a coven Initiation.

For a student who is an adolescent and not ready for Initiation, a ritual affirmation or renewal or a deepening of a student's commitment might be appropriate. Most Sunday school teachers don't end up later ordaining their students, but teachers of Wicca may well do so. To the extent we believe that we are all, inherently, priests or priestesses of the Goddess and God, we need to

Making this painted Altar was a First-Degree task. Seasonal colors and Sabbat illustrations around a spider web decorate, and demonstrate knowledge.

encourage students who feel called, and we must not be afraid to *create* the rites we need.

Self-Dedication

A Self-Dedication might be entirely private, something adolescent or young adult announces that they have performed, or it might be a private rite witnessed by Elders. When undertaken by one of your students or children, Self-Dedication should be celebrated, and gifted, with the proviso that the gift be something encouraging, inviting the novice to "keep on keepin' on." Consider, too, (with the youth's or maiden's permission) sending an announcement to your local newsletter, and to *Circle* or other regional newsletters and magazines.

A Self-Dedication may be the first full ritual students compose. One approach they might take is to dedicate one appropriate aspect of themselves to each Quarter, and ask that Quarter for support in another aspect that needs bolstering. Students ready for Self-Dedication are going to have some ideas already; if there are any Traditional elements they need to include, or anything they should avoid, now's the time to say so!

The growth of children quintessentially symbolizes what we worship, it seems to us, and merits great devotional attention. Our ancestors observed rites and performed rituals for the needs and circumstances of their lives, and so must we. We preach *strength through diversity* and *infinite possibilities*, so we need to honor and value that diversity and those possibilities. That means *recognizing* them and truly *celebrating* them in our students' and children's lives.

Sun Day School

As I've said, we think of raising a child as an act of magic—sacred and requiring much care. So, in talking about raising Witches, it makes sense to start where we would in working magic: with the preparations. Assuming you're already familiar with the preparations required for having children, we'll look at the preparations we think are required for teaching Wicca to them.

Before you have any *Sun Day School* flyers printed, there are lots of things you need to think about. Exactly what those things are—beyond the administrative and logistic challenges all such projects face—depends on who *you* are. What families, covens, and communities need to do to get ready to teach children will vary.

The details of your approach also depend on where you live, what resources are available to you, and what local challenges you face. These kinds of circumstances change, and we need to take local attitudes into account when we plan to teach our children (of any age) about the Craft. We haven't developed a universal checklist, but we'll address some of the things we think are important. You need to think about your situation and make your own checklist!

No matter how formally or informally you're planning to teach, and no matter how many children or what age group you're working with, it's appropriate to give your endeavor some structure. Our Circles and our understanding of "astral physics" give our magic its structure. We can structure our teaching just as secular teachers do, borrowing some concepts that are not hard to understand even if you don't have a formal background in education.

Plenty of people use the words "curriculum," "syllabus," and "lesson plan" interchangeably, and that's the root of considerable confusion. Once we're clear that each of those words names a different aspect of the process of teaching, it all becomes clearer.

The word "curriculum" (Latin) refers (per my poor old *Webster's New World Dictionary*, 1960) to "a specific course of study or, collectively, all the courses of study in a school, university, etc." The word "syllabus" (Greek) means "a summary or outline containing the main points, especially of a course of study." Curricula and syllabi (the words' plural forms) help you develop focused lessons and offer a framework for older students' participation in lesson planning. A syllabus written to each element of the curriculum helps clarify your subject. (That's different from "knowing your material." It means being quite sure about the focus of the class, and knowing what material does *not* belong in the syllabus, as well as what material does.)

A lesson plan specifies what you're going to teach, how you're going to teach it, and—this is pretty important—how you're going to decipher whether or not the child has learned the lesson. Mind you, written tests are not the only way to measure students' understanding. However, challenging students to demonstrate what they have learned is time—and nature—honored. Well and appropriately designed "tests" are joyful discoveries of what students have learned.

So, a curriculum tells you what categories of information you're presenting, a syllabus tells you what specific pieces of information you're going to include from those categories, and a lesson plan tells you how you're going to present those pieces of information and how you're going to know you've gotten them across. We think it's wise to work out your curriculum and a syllabus, and at least the first few lesson plans, for practice and for starters, before you print up the flyers. Some people work better by plunging in with more enthusiasm than preparation, and when it works, that's an example of strength through diversity. When it doesn't, it means you should try another approach.

Other examples follow, but I'll start by suggesting ways to write age-appropriate syllabi for a six-topic curriculum.

	Infancy	**Early Childhood**
History	good memories of comfort and safety.	Gardner is father of Wicca.
Thealogy/ Cosmology	Be gentle, no violence.	Mother Earth and Seasons; Green Man
Ethics	Be gentle, no violence	Always ask; how to vent acceptably
Ritual	Dance, chant, incense, music.	Correct Circle behavior.
Lore	Songs.	Stories.
Magic	Somebody comes every time baby cries.	Reality checks on fairy-tale magic, focus on Nature's magic such as buds in Spring.

	Later Child-hood	Adolescence	Young Adult-hood
History	Developments since the 1950s	Paleo information.	About controversy.
Thealogy/ Cosmology	Triple Goddess grain and game God.	Comparative religions.	In-depth on various topics.
Ethics	Rede and Law; authority and responsibility.	Fate, free will, "karma."	Ethics of spell-casting.
Ritual	Elements and purpose of ritual, difference between Sabbats and Esbats; first Dedication?	Comparative ritual & increasing participation, Manning or Womaning?	Creating and collecting tools; Traditional lore, etc.; if on an initiatory track; gatherings.
Lore	More stories and how stories work.	Comparative lore.	Researching lore, memorizing or writing stories or songs.
Magic	Difference between wishes, dreams, tantrums, etc., and real magic, simple "energy running" and visualization.	Comparative types of magic, various cultural and community styles; more about ethics, authority & responsibility.	Magical physics and basic correspondences; develop specialty or outline a research project.

Sometimes the best-written lesson plans go awry. Sometimes it's because something wonderful happens and the planned lesson is happily abandoned to take advantage of whatever is going on. Sometimes it's because somebody, maybe you, messed up. Make an "executive decision," up front, that it's okay to make a few mistakes. You're going to be working with children, and in some respects beyond the joke, it really is their job to make mistakes. (If you're working with adults, you know they need even more comforting.) If you're going to convince any of them that their mistakes don't doom them, you need to get past feeling doomed by yours.

Sometimes, we feel as mistakes things that *aren't* mistakes. For example, sometimes TAWN has a Moon School, and sometimes it doesn't. How many members have children who are interested is one determining factor; how many members are interested in teaching is another; what resources are available is yet another. Something else that can change is a group's membership's ideas about what the group should be doing. But it's not useless to develop a curriculum, or aspects of a curriculum. That can be on hand when need supports the idea of a Moon School. Better our teachers have "too many" resources than not enough resources. If you have ideas, clarify and develop them, and make them available to your community. The worst that can happen is that you'll have helped the future, and that's actually a good thing.

Teaching styles are at least as different as learning styles, and of course, the subject matter has something to do with how we teach, too. No matter what our teaching style is or how hard we worked to develop it, we need to remember that it's the *religion* we're trying to impress upon the children, not our own brilliance. Teachers need to check in, now and again, to make sure the lessons are getting across and making sense.

Whether or not you use written tests, talk to your students and work with them to their capabilities. Even if they can memorize and recite what you said, or answer test questions correctly, converse with them—dance in a circle with them—and get a feel for if and how they're understanding you. Keep records of these conversations so that you can stay in touch with how much you've accomplished!

Records of your interaction with your children or students may also suggest other effective approaches to your material, may highlight an interest that can be pursued, or suggest a metaphor for relating ideas in new ways. There are lots of "education" books about teaching techniques and methods, and some of them are helpful. There are many other books inventorying various creative projects that can be independent activities or put in the context of specific lessons. One of your best resources for teaching Wicca is *your students*. Listen to their questions, and help them be patient, but rejoice in their impatience to learn!

It's generally good when the *way* you teach kind of matches the *material* you're teaching. Witchcraft teaches us that life is an adventure, so it's alright for its teaching to *be* an adventure. For example: You don't teach chants just by writing the words on the board. You have to let your students practice chanting, so they can learn not only the words, but the way it feels to chant, and to hear live chanting, and to be part of a group creating something beyond themselves by chanting.

Where we live, public classes (for grown-ups, but children have attended with their parents) are offered by a British Traditional priest, often more than once a year, through the Open University. The lessons are designed to give a broad view of the Craft's diversity, and emphasize the similarities among the Traditions, while celebrating their distinctions. We recommend them to newcomers to the Craft (and the Craft in Tucson); we took the Explorer to them several times. (The instructor was concerned that some material was "too adult" for a 5- or 6-year old, though we found none of it objectionable. His problem was moral, but in some places, it would've been legal. If the law in your state says children can't look at slides of naked bottoms or the occasional naked breast, or at a Maypole, roll your eyes and moan, but don't take any chances.

Before You Print Up the Flyers

- ❧ Who will you be teaching? How many children? Is your child one of them?
- ❧ How old are they? Are you working with a same-age group, or a multigenerational crowd? How do they get along? How do they feel about all this?
- ❧ Who will be doing the teaching? Parents? Elders? A team? Several people from the community? The same people every time? Guest speakers occasionally?
- ❧ How do the children you're working with learn best? Through physical activity? Through craft projects? Through visual media? Through audio media? In traditional classroom or other formal situations? One-on-one? In learning pairs or teams? By focusing intensely on one aspect of a subject at a time? By understanding a wide context first?
- ❧ What is your idea of the perfect teaching situation for your circumstances? Have you shared this vision with others? Have you heard anyone else's ideas? Can you support other ideas that the community would like to try? How close to your ideal can you come, and how can you do this?

That last question asks you to think about all the mundane tasks such as counting the kids, talking to their parents, talking to group community leaders, creating a syllabus and lesson plans, finding a space, rounding up some blackboards and chalk, researching the subjects, preparing the hand-outs, etc. The questions that come before it should be helpful to you in defining the scope of your teaching.

In many public schools these days, the first order of the day is to keep the students under control. *Our* emphasis has to be on the truth of the Craft, and not on power-over our students. Fortunately, the circumstances in which we educate our children to the Craft don't involve similar security concerns (though we still have to look out for custody suits). But we run into power-over trouble, too, because Wiccans sometimes have trouble saying no to each other.

Saying No

Would it break your heart to kick angelic little Phaedra out of class this week because she's licked and stuck no less than five lollipops in Jasmine's hair? Could you banish a junior-high-schooler because she or he can't stop making smart-aleck remark during a presentation or a discussion? Could you recommend to Sunrise's parents that they hold off another year until he has better social skills, or suggest they talk to his doctor because he hasn't got the control of body or attention that other children his age have?

How would it feel to be little Jasmine, or her mother, or the shaggy haired boy on the other side of Phaedra (who couldn't listen to the lesson because he had to keep an eye on Phaedra)? Imagine being a parent who hears that at Sun Day School today, we learned that Teacher loses it after Billy pretends, for the sixth time, to see a squirrel up the side of the tree. Sunrise's parents might be awfully angry if you suggest there's anything "wrong" with their darling. You have to know where you stand about mentioning such things. You need to be clear and confident about the limits you set on class behavior, too.

You may be working with children you've known for years, maybe all their lives, and whose families you know. You care about these children to begin with, so when you teach, you're bound to feel some responsibility to and for them as individuals; but it doesn't end there. It doesn't even end with your responsibility to all the children as a whole, or to any group that sponsors, supports, or shares your teaching effort. When you teach Wicca, you're not working for the children, you're not working for the group or community, you're working for the God and the Goddess. Your first responsibility is to Them....so?

So, when a child (of any age, including the ones who look like grown-ups) is disruptive, you need to go into "priestess or priest" or "administrative" mode and deal with it quickly, firmly, and matter-of-factly. Otherwise, you risk enabling that child's disruptive behavior, and that does him a disservice, too. Call it what you will—if you want to teach Wicca, you have to know much more than your "stuff." Just like when you do magic, you have to know a lot more than the correspondences. Of course, it's not all that often that disruptive children—or parents, or neighbors—will be a serious problem; it's only our cultural reluctance to say no that makes it such a big deal.

Once you've got your curriculum and your syllabus and a few lesson plans ready, and once you've laid the behavioral ground rules and worked out the class schedule, what happens? Apart from having enough construction paper or a slide screen without a rip in it, what else can you do to get ready?

There is still some controversy among Wiccans and other Neo-Pagans about how to teach Pagan children their religions. There are time constraints: how often and how long you will be able to meet will influence what you can teach. The make-up of the community will be a factor, too, as we've already seen. But no matter how you approach the subject of religious education for Neo-Pagan youth, you have to get it reasonably well organized before you begin.

The first children you teach will be your own, because you're the one who'll hear their first questions. Canyondancer and I have developed some material about answering "the hard questions," and we offer it as raw material for you to develop as you share your religion with your own children and the community's children.

There is no one Witch of any Tradition who can say, once and for all, what's always right and what's always wrong. Following Wicca, we trust our instincts and rely upon our experience and each other. Wiccan principles and tenets offer us guidelines and encouragement to answer the hard questions for ourselves, and to respect other people's different answers and decisions, because our diversity nourishes us.

Wicca's cosmology acknowledges, in our worship of a generative and eternal Goddess and a God who dies and is reborn, the complimentary nature of matter and energy in the various forms which compose the universe. Wholeness and Individuality are the poles between which energy dances, and they are both—with everything in between—worthy of appreciation and celebration.

In the beauty of Earth's landscapes, in the power of our uninhibited feelings, in the diversity of life, in the universal pattern of birth, growth, death, and rebirth, and in the depth of our wonder, we find our guidance and comfort, our "chapters and verses." We recognize Nature as sacred, and ourselves as part of Nature, so we feel no separation from deity. "Thou art God/dess," we say to each other. Wicca has no need to call anyone a sinner; mortality is not immoral or a punishment, and the Lady and Lord love us all unconditionally. Incarnation does not separate us from the Gods, and we do not look at life as a vale of tears—no, no! We see a grotto of growth!

Reincarnation is a tenet of Wicca; and if you ask 12 Witches how it works, you're likely to get 13 answers! The understanding we all have in common, though, is that we will be back around again, one way or another. We also know that what we do in one life affects all our others, but our ideas about "karma" are not vengeful or punitive. We're not trying to get "good enough" to be excused from coming back again, either: rebirth is simply "the way the universe works," just as gravity is "the way the universe works."

Wicca is a religion of experience rather than dogma: we have no commandments, but the Wiccan Rede and the Threefold Law capsulize the "rules" we affirm across all our Traditions: "An ye harm none, do as ye will," and, "What you put into the World(s) returns to you threefold." Because we are conscious of a kinship with the rest of life, our considerations of "harm" and "none" are very wide indeed. We have no fear of our Gods, and no sense of "mereness." We trust in the bits we don't know or remember about life, and that trust in generated by our love for the bits we do know. We're not threatened by other peoples' religions and cultures being different from ours, because life, like a field of flowers, is more beautiful for its great variety. (Thorns? Sure there are thorns, but they don't make the roses less lovely, they only remind us to be careful.)

Guided by these ideas, Wiccans look to the inner truth for answers to the hard questions. We are never asked to deny our fears or angers, but we are responsible for transforming those energies and using them constructively in our own lives and in the world. This transformation is the heart of magic, and the heart of the Craft. If there *were* a single answer to the hard questions, it would be "transformation." There are no "pat" answers, but there's a pat on the back for finding your own answers.

Wicca, with its trust in the sacred nature of life and its confidence of the God's and Goddess's unconditional love, lets us appreciate everything about our mortal experience and gives us guilt-free answers to the hard questions. The basic tenets of the Craft—that the Goddess and God represent the complementary polarities of the universe, the belief in magic and reincarnation, the idea of the Web of Wyrd that binds us all to one another—empower us with responsibility (rather than blame) for our lives. It is from this perspective that we approach life's challenges and consider these, fairly standard hard questions.

Why am I alive?

Well, Mommy and Daddy love each other very much, and...Or, the Big Bang was material, and the Goddess's creation of consciousness is spiritual. It is the nature of the universe/Goddess to be alive and creative.

Okay, but what are we supposed to do about it?

We're supposed to do as we will, and we harm none. We're supposed to ask naught of sacrifice and love all beings. The purpose of life is life and its experience!

Why do bad things happen? Am *I* bad if I do a bad thing or a bad thing happens to me?

No! "Bad" things may be the consequences of hasty or unfocused choices, fear, or ignorance, or chemical imbalance; sometimes they are beyond human control. There's a difference between things you do wrong and things that happen to you. If you do something wrong, take responsibility and make up for it if you can, and if you can't pay it back, then pay it forward. When "bad" things happen, on purpose or on accident, they raise energy, and that energy can still be turned to good work.

Why did someone I love do a bad thing?

From fear, most likely, or ignorance. There are chemically imbalanced brains, and fear can be just as crippling as any physical injury or disease. Fear and ignorance are behind every hurtful behavior.

Is there divine punishment for wrong-doing?

None is needed. For most physical-plane crimes, there are material consequences. With the God and Goddess, there is only the healing, only the learning, only the experience of Wholeness. Love unto all beings is the Law of the Goddess, and the chant reminds us that "where there is love, there can be no fear." Responsibility remains, and civil or criminal penalties may reasonably be imposed. But spiritually, guilt and punishment are destructive, not creative, and more destruction won't build character.

How should I respond to people who do bad things?

First, restrain them if that's necessary, and get yourself to safety. Calm their fears and yours. Teaching and healing are easier if you love them anyway, and don't take it personally. (Obviously we are not talking about extremely violent crimes here; don't take chances: call 9-1-1 if you need to.)

How should we handle our own fears?

Acknowledge them, and then inform them so that they aren't unrealistic. For instance: you won't fall off the world if you go to Australia; you won't catch AIDS from hugging somebody; normally, people will speak to you again after what you did or didn't do. On the other hand, it's good to be afraid of sticking your hands into an old woodpile and having something venomous or rabid bite you, because that's not at all unlikely! Work with the energy of fear to spin it into something constructive.

What about this sex business, anyway?

Sex is only bad when it is a business. There is no natural conflict between our hormones and our higher selves; yet some pleasures and parts are so special we want those we share them with to be equally special. Everybody's body is beautiful and deserves respect. Sex isn't all there is to love, and not all love is sexual. Sex is good, very good, but it's not worth dying for.

Why do some people think we're Satanists? Why can't I talk about Wicca?

Once upon a time, when Christian armies were expanding their empires, they found that native Pagan people didn't want to be conquered. The only way to replace Pagan religions with Christianity was to lie about Paganism and kill the Pagans who resisted. There are fewer swords drawn against us these days, but people still believe the same lies. People won't believe them forever, but not everybody's ready to hear the truth yet.

Um, what about death? What happens when I die?

Your body is cremated or buried to return it to the Earth. Your soul returns to the womb of the Goddess, "like a drop of rain, flowing to the ocean," as the chant goes. Through the Mother we are all reborn many times, as the God shows us in His yearly cycle. "To love you must be born, and to be born, you must die," some Wiccan Initiation rites confide. It's sad never to see somebody again in this lifetime, but it doesn't have to be scary. Death is not a punishment, it's the beginning of rebirth. Only bodies die; love never does.

Exactly how you present these premises and points to your children depends only partly on your child's age and ability to understand. It depends very much on which are the hardest questions for you. It's good to learn, with your children, things like state capitals and assorted crafts, even about effective behavior in the world. It is not good to work through your own childhood issues in your child's life. (It's good to work them out, though, and it's good to see when you're working them out inappropriately, and to find a better way.)

If it's difficult for at least some grown-ups, individually, to sort through basic thealogical questions, it's hard for groups, too. The bigger the group, the greater the effort required to agree on the basics. For some communities, agreeing, in theory, that organizing a Sun Day or Moon School is the easy part. Coming to agreement on a specific core curriculum might pose more challenges. Where do you start?

Well, you start here, by reading this and other books and otherwise networking with other people who have experience and ideas. You do your homework (fair enough, right?) and use as much as you can of what you find. With the energy you save not trying to reinvent the wheel, you can focus on identifying and marshaling the resources available to you.

You can read about successful teaching techniques in all kinds of education books, but there are very few specifically Wiccan or Neo-Pagan books about teaching. There are very few books that offer support for Wiccan and Neo-Pagan Sun Day School programs. If any Traditions of Wicca have developed specific materials and techniques for teaching their children, they're not public. Many Traditions decline to take students younger than 16 or 18 years old, even if they are Pagan children. More and more Wiccans, though, are interested in teaching their children more deliberately than casual opportunities may allow.

It makes sense to us to focus on history, thealogy, cosmology, ethics, ritual, lore, and magic. Developing a consistent curriculum from these categories establishes some guidelines and should help keep the presentations balanced. Of course, you don't present the same material in the same way you present it to older kids or teens as you would to young children. Fortunately, what we can teach about Wicca is quite a rich body of information and lore, and lends itself to being understood on several levels.

We introduced the Explorer to the Gods first by Their simplest names: Mother Nature and Father Time. In fact, the Adventure Tradition does not recognize a (capital F) Father aspect of the God, but children can't understand distinctions like that until they're much, much older. As the Explorer grew, we introduced him to other aspects of the Lady and Lord, so that his understanding matured as he did. A Sun Day or Moon School would need to offer its curriculum in different forms for children of various age groups. Especially if you can't meet at least once a week, it'll be the "6years old and older" crowd that responds best to information, while the younger ones will do better with an emphasis on activities.

Here's a suggestion for the sort of "small-c" craft program you might want for those younger than 6. (Cauldron-lucks are what TAWN calls its pot-luck meetings, Fall Fest is TAWN's annual open-to-the-public Mabon festival, and "luminarias" are, in this case, punched tin candleholders.)

- January: macaroni necklaces—significance of ritual jewelry in Neo-Pagan religions.
- February: construction paper Valentines—ways we know the Goddess loves us.
- March: Ostara baskets—seed packets and egg-carton planters.
- April: construction paper (pre-cut shapes and colors) collages of favorite animals—animal correspondences.
- May: Maypole—color correspondences or kinds of creativity (making babies, dancing, baking, understanding new ideas, etc).
- June: flavored ice cream or slushie making (if no one has a machine, rent one)—this could be fund-raising for Moon School field-trips, too—and bits of flavorful cooking herb lore
- July: pool party at someone's house after cauldron-luck. BBQ and fireworks (if legal in your state). Talk about freedom and responsibility and tolerance of other people's religions and about citizenship.
- August: games! If it's too hot for foot races and such, then quieter games and the prizes are specially-baked/flavored loaves of bread. (Lugh established games in his mother's name at Lughnassadh. The word "Lammas" comes from the Anglo-Saxon

for loaf-mass.) Ask parents to save tin cans for October's activity.

✌ September: making masks on the theme of the Fall Fest's costume contest. Talk about the theme, and about community. Remind parents about tin cans for October's activity. Remind kids and parents to bring a donation for the Food Bank to Fall Fest.

✌ October: decorating tin cans (any size) to make luminarias. Talk about the darkness of Winter and ways our beliefs can light our way.

✌ November: construction paper turkeys. Discuss the ways that feasts are communions, how we're all inter-related, etc.

✌ December: 11"x17" construction paper Yule banners. Talk about Yule customs and their origins.

You have to take the attention span of your students into account, and be prepared to structure your lessons not just to "get around it," but to take advantage of it. If little kids need to get up and run around every 20 minutes (and they do), then come up with some running exercises or games that reinforce what you've just been teaching.

Reinforcing Your Lessons

Early in childhood and later, through adolescence and into young adulthood, kids like to move; sometimes they just can't help it. Here are some examples of physical activity that can reinforce or expand on many Craft lessons:

✌ If you're talking about Celtic myths, re-enact the Lughnassadh games Lugh established in honor of his mother; if you're studying Goddesses, run like Artemis through the forest.

✌ If you're talking about quests, set up a scavenger hunt.

✌ If you're talking about challenges, take a deep breath and line up a tug-of-war. Play charades.

- ❧ If you're working on concentration and visualization, try a human chess game, or checkers.
- ❧ Play a game of freeze tag and let the kids speculate on what it means.

Generally speaking, for younger children, look at fewer subjects. Once kids are verbal, you can talk to them about almost anything, but the younger they are, the simpler you have to keep the subjects. The Explorer soon outgrew his first understanding of the Goddess and God as Mother Nature and Father Time, but those simplifications got him started. (Remembering these earliest names did not confuse him later, when he learned that our Tradition does not see the Lord as a "Father.") We told him that these were names of "those we worship," (that's just about all we told him) because that's all he wanted to know. We left it to him, in his own time and experience, to get some ideas about what those names meant, and what worship was (beyond the Circle experience).

We find that you can trust children to ask you about the things they're trying to understand, and that you can often tell by what and how they're asking what aspect of the answer they're looking for. We all know the story about little Billie coming home to ask her parents where she came from, which prompted from them the whole birds-and-bees story. When she still looked puzzled at the end of that story, her parents asked what she still didn't understand. Little Billie was wondering where she came from because Adelina came from Pittsburgh. (It's only cute when it happens to somebody else.) When you're teaching children you know, pay attention to their body language and their *psyche* language as well.

You will notice that you have more information than you can give your students. This is good. Their challenge is to learn; yours is to categorize what you know usefully so you can give the children what they are able to apprehend. Introduce new material gradually, and let the children themselves pick up the pace by *asking* for more information when they're ready to learn more or faster.

Pay attention to any specific comments children make when you talk to them about organizing classes. Making notes is not a

bad idea. If you're attentive to their interests, and if you integrate those interests with the other subjects you teach, then
you will have more willing students. Then, in addition to teaching
Wicca, you're teaching a love of learning, which is one of our
primal gifts from the Gods, one we can be proud to instill in our
children. This doesn't mean you let children tell you what to
teach, only that you can take advantage of their interests to
relate your lessons to their lives.

Our practical model of the cosmos (many Wiccans, but not
all, use it) is the Anglo-Saxon Web of Wyrd, which posts intricate, multi-dimensional, and virtually infinite interconnections.
As above, so below: in the structure of the universe we have the
Web connecting everything, and in the structure of our brains
we have the corpus callosum connecting everything. We think
that's...Significant. As science reaches for its unified field theory,
so we reach for ours. Whatever we teach, it has to be consistent
with a fundamental cognizance of it all.

There's a lot to consider—and undoubtedly much to resolve—
when you decide on formally teaching Wicca to children: you
could call it a daunting task. Dividing this big job into several
easier-to-handle little ones, here are five tips that summarize how
to organize Craft classes for children:

1.   Be specific about what you're teaching. Create
      a curriculum and make a syllabus and lesson
      plan, and keep your students' attention spans
      in mind when you do.

2.   Remember that you don't have to teach
      everything all at once.

3.   Think about how to present the material most
      effectively.

4.   Your course might introduce students to a
      variety of topics in an overview, or concentrate
      on one or two elements of thealogy or magic.

5. Know the boundaries of the material you're offering; know what does *not* get class time.

Your curriculum is the backbone of your educational program. It tells you what you're going to teach, what subjects you feel your students need to learn in order to understand Wicca. If you plan to teach history, thealogy and cosmology, ethics, ritual, lore, and magic, then those six subjects *are* your curriculum.

A syllabus gets a little more specific: What history are you teaching? Ancient? Modern? What rituals will you tell them about? Sabbats? Moons? Passages? All of them? In creating a syllabus for each of the topics in the curriculum, there's a risk of implying that each of those topics should be taught separately. We think it's much more realistic to integrate them, but this must be done differently for different age groups.

History

When we talk about teaching Wicca's history, we run into some difficulty immediately. What is Wicca's history? (See **Burning Times** in the Glossary.) One solution to this problem, particularly with younger children who aren't yet interested in the academics, is to teach Wicca's modern history. To say that Gardner founded modern Wicca doesn't pass judgment on earlier times. The "history" component of your curriculum can be greatly simplified for young children ("Gerald Gardner is the grandfather of Wicca" might be all you need to say. If you can show them a picture, he'll stick in their minds!) There's plenty of room to expand the topic for older children.

For older children, a brief overview of the variety of Wiccan Traditions and when they developed, characterized in just a few sentences, is appropriate. Adolescents can begin to explore other Pagan religions, and the paths of Asatru and Druidism can be introduced, along with their histories. Young adults, as I've suggested, can read Hutton and other serious scholarship, and perhaps undertake research projects themselves.

Thealogy/Cosmology

What do we believe about deity and how the spiritual c
magical universe works? Young children seem to do well with th
concept of Mother Earth, and introducing the God as Fathe
Time is also an option. With young children, the most importar
lesson to convey is that the Goddess and God love us uncond
tionally, even when we get hurt or scared or make mistakes. Th
gods are not threatening. The Wheel won't be fully understoo
by the youngest, but they'll enjoy seeing the illustrations an
learning to make seasonal associations.

Older children can begin to understand that the Goddess an
God aren't a big lady and a big man who live in the clouds. They wi
naturally wonder about how things work—and the difference be
tween *make-believe* and *real* magic needs to be made clear. Their sens
of time is developing nicely now, so more work on the Wheel
appropriate. Adolescents and young adults can discuss the Wheel
symbolism in still greater depth, and explore various aspects of th
Wiccan Goddess and God, as well as exploring other Neo-Pagai
religions more thoroughly.

Ethics

In a brochure about the basics of Wicca distributed by Mothe
Earth Ministries-ATC, a Pagan prison ministry I work for, ethics
the first thing we talk about. It's the first thing we mention whei
we're teaching people new to the Craft, too. When we're teachin
kids, it should be part of everything else we teach, but the subjec
needs specific attention, as well. Young children can begin by learn
ing that you don't touch anybody's Altar or Tools or jewelry withou
asking and getting permission first.

Older children can start to understand the magical or astra
reasoning behind our ethical rules. It's also appropriate to discus
the rules other religions follow, and notice both similarities an
differences. Adolescents and young adults are likely to want to tall
about very particular situations as they work on sorting out the fas
and furious changes in their lives.

Ritual

Young children like to dance and they enjoy holding hands and moving in circles; but they also like to say no because it's a very powerful word. The many parents (us and our coveners included) who let their children play freely in and around Circles know that children's attention wanders. If you want to introduce them to Circles a little more formally than once a month in the family room or backyard, start slow. With very young kids, forming a circle by holding hands is an accomplishment itself! As children get older, they can understand the concepts of Quarters, and can start to learn about tools.

Older children are ready to learn more about ritual forms, and may be interested in creating ritual themselves, or contributing ideas. Subtler points can be introduced now—the difference between invoking and inviting and between dismissing and thanking. Adolescents may be ready to take some part in ritual. Campsight usually asks an adolescent girl to be the Maiden at our Yule ritual because it's one of relatively few ritual roles that can be giggled and blushed through without disrupting the rest of the rite. Young adults should be ready to understand the broadest and most abstract implications of ritual, and, if they're working toward coven membership, they can start memorizing specific ritual elements and forms.

Lore

Lore can be explained to little children as "stories." There are plenty of sources, and young children will enjoy anything from the Cerridwen and Gwion story (if it's told so as not to scare them half to death) to any of the wonderful children's stories available at bookstores today. Older children can begin to cope with some more specific stories—ranging from fairy tales to tales of the Burning Times. Older children are also ready to hear family and community stories. Adolescents and young adults can work with Wicca's lore by retelling familiar stories, and by telling their own life story in mythical terms. They're also ready for any non-Oath-bound Traditional lore, including any skills your Tradition teaches.

Magic

Young children, and even older ones, need more reassurance that they're *not* making things happen in the world than that they are. What they need to be sure of is that the rules of magic will keep them from doing harm inadvertently. As they get older, they're ready to start learning various energy techniques, like visualization and memorization. They are able to understand more, and more complex, correspondences as well. They can also begin to learn about chakras, and short guided meditations are also appropriate. Older children are ready to start keeping journals, an easy way to develop the discipline that magic requires.

Adolescents are ready to learn that there are different kinds of magic, and that sometimes, things "just happen." Various theories of magical physics can be introduced to them, too. Young adults may be ready to work magic on their own, but they're probably not ready to improvise without supervision. They may be interested in research projects, too, on a variety of topics.

Later Childhood: Syllabus for Six Sessions

Here's a sample syllabus for six sessions with children between the ages of 6 and 11:

1st session	Intro to Craft as real religion, different from popular images (history).
2nd session	Goddess and God, how we think about Nature (thealogy/cosmology).
3rd session	Where does everything come from and go? Mention of Summerland and reincarnation

4th session   When Witches meet, what we do when we meet, and the need for secrecy (ritual, lore).

5th session   Spells, charms, amulets, etc., "good" and "bad" magic, intro Law and Rede (ethics, magic).

6th session   Review of Craft as real religion, different traditions, public still learning (history; ethics; the future).

Your lesson plan is basically your "order of lesson," and in addition to specifying exactly what you're going to talk about, you have to give some thought to *how* you'll present what you're teaching. Will you have guest speakers? Go on field trips? Show slides or films? Will you wear robes or street clothes? Will you use an opening ritual? Will you need room to pace? Do you like to use a blackboard? Poster-boards? Handouts? Reading assignments? Writing assignments?

Some assignments measure themselves—book reports and "make something" projects, for instance. Others—like enjoying a slide show or listening to someone read—don't. You have to think about how you're going to find out whether or not the children learned what you wanted them to learn. It's great to get the *did-you-all-have-a-good-time-today-YES!* kind of feedback, but having a good time and grasping a concept are two different things. As a teacher (and priestess or priest too, quite likely), you need to care more about their grasping the concepts than liking you.

For ideas about creative "testing" and how to know that your test is testing what you want to test, check with...your local librarian. She'll help you find some useful books. You can also talk to secular teachers for ideas and suggestions of books to look at. It's some trouble, but aren't your kids worth it? Isn't Wicca?

Sample Lesson Plan:
Session Three (one hour)

A lesson plan derived from our sample syllabus is laid out below.

- ❧ Show commercial calendars that include some Pagan holidays and the phases of the Moon; introduce Wheel of Year.

- ❧ Show illustrations (slides, pictures from books, pictures from your coven's scrapbook) of Sabbats and Esbats; discuss celebrations at Festivals and magic at Moons. Break for refreshments, after talking about Cakes and Ale.

- ❧ If Craft is about Nature that everybody can see, why do we have to keep it a secret? Talk about different kinds of secrets and that some can't be shared because other people aren't ready to understand them. Reassure students that they don't have to keep icky secrets.

- ❧ Close with a group hug, and be available to answer questions or facilitate further discussion for another few minutes (whenever possible).

We think it's important to plan ahead. Figure out what you need before you start teaching. For the sample lesson above, you'd need a way to illustrate not only the Wheel of the Year, but Sabbat and Esbat activities, and you need some snacks. You might be comfortable with a black board, some colored chalk, and a copy of a book that has nice illustrations. You might rather create a poster board or other visual aide. You might be able to use an overhead or a slide projector. Maybe you'd like to include music; maybe you'll want to get the kids into a practice circle. All that's up to you!

Prepare for your classes as you would for ritual. Give it the same respect. It's not a play-date, for you or them. The right time for children to go off on flights of fancy about Wicca is after they understand the basics. Think about all kinds of things rom glue and construction paper and scissors to a globe, from ides and pictures to a place to meet and refreshments. Make sts. You even have to think about how much it's going to cost nd whether students (well, probably their parents) will need to elp cover that cost.

Having a curriculum established, and syllabi for each age roup, will be of enormous help in the task of sorting out what ou need to teach which lessons. It's less effective to try orga- izing Sun Day or Moon Schools around the "stuff" you just appen to have on hand. There is only so much you can do with litter, glue, and popsicle sticks! However, it's a good idea to be lexible in planning young children's activities, so that you can ake advantage of what "stuff" people happen to have on hand nd are willing to donate.

Another good idea—appropriate on just about any level ou can think of—is to get other people to help. If you're teach- ng children other than your own, you need their parents' per- nission, of course, but you also need their support and ontributions. Someone in the community might have *just* what ou need, so publish a wish list or call for help on flyers or in a ewsletter. Ask local Witches to come and work with your stu- lents. Likewise, ask for suggestions and guest speakers for field rips to the zoo, the botanical gardens or arboretum, to a local itual site, or somebody's house who has a neat altar they can ell you about and let you admire.

We're an experiential religion, so our teaching is more along he line of making certain experiences possible and providing a ontext in which to understand them Yes, of course, sometimes ou'll lecture or otherwise present information pretty straight- orwardly. But it's not supposed to be somebody standing at the ront imparting knowledge and grace to assembled sinners. When ve lecture, we should be talking about our subject because we're assionate about it and it's meaningful and inspiring to us.

It's been shown that many of us learn more and remember t better when the lesson is associated with at least three senses. Ve can see and hear the teacher, but taking notes or practicing

a dance step or singing amplifies the input, and makes it mor
likely that what we've learned will stick with us. Human being
learn in plenty of ways—some of us best by listening, others b
reading, others by doing—and we need to present our teaching
in as many of those modes as we can, to give our students th
best chance of finding meaning in them.

Finally, keep a journal. You'll learn more from your exper
ence if you can refer to your notes, where you will undoubtedl
find material of great practical value, too. Your experience wi
greatly enlarge your community's resources, as well, so your note
will be helpful to other teachers.

Some Traditions teach their children intentionally and com
munally, but the idea is still new to most Wiccans. It's an exercis
of creativity, considering what to teach and how to teachWicc
to the children in our communities. Our way of thinking distir
guishes us as Pagans, and it can distinguish us as teachers, too.

Here are some guidelines for developing syllabi from a curricu
lum, some charts to work with. Think about the relationships the
imply. Use them to make explorations of Witchcraft more interes
ing, to provoke thought about Wiccan philosophies, attitudes, an
approaches to life, and to enhance your and your students' exper
ences of the Craft as religion and lifestyle. The blank spaces a
invitations to fill in the blanks yourself. Charts and lists for yc

	Ages 1-5	*Ages 6-11*	*Ages 12-15*	*Ages 16+*
Deity	Mother Earth	Lord and Lady	comparative	personal choices
Calendar	seasons, Moons	Sabbats		
Ethics	not wihtout asking	Rede and Law		

and your students to finish are like guided meditations for your *left* brain. These make good teaching devices in vocal groups of older children, adolescents, and young adults, and they can be helpful tools in teaching adult apprentices in small classes.

As you read, you'll come up with lots of your own ideas, both generally and specifically appropriate to your community. New examples and metaphors will occur to you, and new ways of presenting material. This is one way the God and Goddess speak to us, in a carefully thought-out idea and in a sudden and delightful *"Oh!"* These charts present good ideas, but their real use is to inspire you to come up with another, better or more appropriate for your project way to organize and present material to the kids you're teaching. Like any other magic, the more of yourself you put into this, the better it's going to work for you and yours.

Remember that not *all* charts have to be in rows like these. The best way to present information about relationships isn't always in boxes. Some charts need to be round, and some are map-like. Interesting discussions with older students could ensue from a question about the appropriateness of presenting all sorts of information in other sorts of ways. An important distinction to make is between content and style. It's important to get our facts right; it's also important to present them in context, in a style consistent with content. After all, you wouldn't want to sit people down in rows of chairs and just *tell* them about these great circular rituals we do.

	Ages 1-5	*Ages 6-11*	*Ages 12-15*	*Ages 6-11*
To Know		memorize correspon- dence		
To Dare			camping	
To Will				long-term commit- ment
To Be Silent	shhh for a time			

One of the first elements of Wicca we present to our children is the Goddess. Here are some suggestions about which of Her aspects to present at which ages:

- Infancy: This is the age of the Big Bang: a baby's mind goes from not differentiating between self and others, to starting to. Our job is to help babies know they are safe even if Mommy and Daddy are separate people. Attention on demand, to the extent you can manage it, is what a child under the age of 1 really needs, and one of the best investments of time and energy you can make.

- Early Childhood: She is the "Love that cannot be withdrawn;" He is the young child who dares to venture away from Mother because he knows he can always return. The God's journey around the Wheel takes Him far away and then brings Him back close, too.

- Later Childhood: Talk about the deity of Nature and the nature of Deity. Take cues from the children's developing understandings.

- Adolescence: __________
  Fill in this blank with your children or students. Does your Trad or community honor all Goddesses as one Goddess and all Gods as one God, or relate better to deities as full-fledged individuals?

- Young Adulthood: Maybe you're already having regular thealogical and cosmological discussions with your students; if not, start now!

When you undertake to teach the Craft to children, you are both brave and pioneering. To those of you we never meet, we pay our respects and admiration now.

It's hard. You might find resistance within your own Pagan community, and you may come under attack from the public at large if what you are doing is "out of the broom closet." It may be difficult to get started, and people may be indifferent about helping out at first. Then again, everything may go swimmingly. Now, more and more often, it does.

Brave hearts, y'all! Keep the faith, as we used to say, and the faith will keep you. Persist in perfect love and perfect trust, and you will be more of an educator and avatar than you'll ever know.

> Keep the Magic flowing,
> Keep the Circle glowing,
> Keep the Young Ones growing,
> And that's good enough for me!

The end...or is it?

> The children are growing,
> the students are learning;
> the magic is showing,
> the Wheel is turning.
> The Witches are teaching,
> the love is flowing;
> the young ones are reaching,
> the Goddess is glowing.

May everything in this book be fuel for your own inspiration! And may all your own efforts and energy empower you and your children, and all the generations to come. Sing blesséd be, and blesséd be, and blesséd be again!

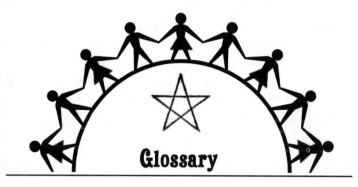

Glossary

Altar(s): The surfaces where we lay out ritual gear in preparation of a Circle. Any place that we lay out sacred items to honor an Element, an Idea, or an Ancestor is also called an Altar. We can also distinguish between formal Altars and working Altars (usually capitalized).

Apprentice: What we call someone who is learning the Craft from a teacher. We also call students of the Craft **Novices** and **Dedicants**.

As above, so below: A way of saying that natural laws apply universally and that our inter-connectedness makes all realms metaphors for one another. As above (the larger system, the macrocosm), so below (the individual system, the microcosm).

Astral: A name for planes or dimensions of experience that exist beyond ordinary understanding and measurement. Some are personal, some are universal.

Athame (*ah-thah-may* or *ath-uh-may*): The ritual knife, usually double-edged, used to cast Circles and for other magical purposes.

Auras: Etheric bodies or force fields, energies that collect around and become part of organic bodies like ours. Kurlean photography is said to picture them. Learning to see or otherwise sense them is not hard, and Diane Stein's book *Stroking the Python* has some good instruction.

B.C.E: means "before the Christian era" or "before the Common Era."

Between the Worlds: Where the Circle puts you, a sacred space that exists in, and can draw energy from, all dimensions.

Beyond the Veil: Another way of referring to that which is beyond what we can see, hear, taste, touch, or know intellectually. Ghosts and the Vastness of Space are both "beyond the veil." "Parting the veil" is a reference to perception beyond the distinction between life and death. Most "religious experiences" are the effect of parting the veil.

Book of Shadows (BOS): What Witches call their handwritten books of ritual, spells, charms, chants, journal entries, meditations, etc. The traditionally black-covered BOS is, as a rule, not shown to the uninitiated.

Burning Times: What Witches call the Inquisition, when throughout most of Europe accused Witches were burned with other heretics. The period lasted for about 500 years, with the fiercest activity taking place from the 15th-17th century. In England, Witches were drowned or hung; they were hung (not burned) here, too. Wiccans must continue to honor our Burning Times lore, but we must also acknowledge new scholarship about it. Ronald Hutton, a British scholar, wrote a book called *The Triumph of the Moon* (Oxford University Press, 1999) which I do not believe we can ignore. I think it's important enough to summarize here, and we strongly recommend that you and your old-enough students read the whole book.